THERE I WAS AND HERE I AM
BY TODD M. HOWE

There I Was and Here I Am

There I Was and Here I Am

TODD M. HOWE

ISBN-13: 9781516841196
ISBN-10: 1516841190

Disclaimer

I have tried to recreate events, locales and conversations from my memories of them. In order to maintain their anonymity in some instances I have changed the names of individuals and places, I may have changed some identifying characteristics and details such as physical properties, occupations and places of residence. Any resemblance to actual persons, living or dead, or actual events, businesses, or places are in fact purely coincidental.

Although I have made every effort to ensure that the information in this book was correct at press time, I do not assume and hereby disclaim any liability to any party for any loss, damage, or disruption caused by errors or omissions, whether such errors or omissions result from negligence, accident, or any other cause.

This story begins with a child who had an impractical and seemingly unattainable secret dream — a secret so deep, he was afraid to admit it to himself and never would admit it to anyone else. This, for fear it might never come true: a young boy from a poor family who wanted to fly airplanes. It takes him from that place to the realization of his dream, along with all the ups and downs of life to get him there.

Table of Content

Preface

Most writers, artists, and sculptures need a muse. In Greek and Roman mythology, a muse is someone who presides over the arts and sciences. Personified as a woman, she is the source of inspiration for a creative artist. I have decided to call my muse, "The Bohemian Maiden." When I was growing up, a Bohemian lifestyle had a certain mystique to it, and many Bohemians were artists and authors. The name, "Maiden" was chosen because my muse needed to have a feminine name, but just one name could never describe her fully. So, she is simply a Maiden – a once must mythical being – a montage of people, times, events, loves in my life, past and present – dreams that were and dreams that are to be. Here, I ask my muse to…

Take me there

Imagine, if you will, a cold winter's dawn, just as the sun is rising. You are surrounded in down, bundled and warm. You breathe in the fresh new morning air and feel alive. You hear the crunching of the snow beneath your feet. There is frost everywhere from the evening before. Then, sunlight hits the crystals of ice and snow, and you see a billion rays of light reflecting all colors. You see and feel all of these senses in just a moment of time.

Or, walking down an old country road, kicking dust out from under your feet. You feel the warmth of the dappled sun on your neck and smell the flowers and trees in the bloom of their season. You pick an apple from a nearby tree and taste its delicious sweetness and warmth. You are young, without a care in the world. The summer is yours.

Or, the security you felt when your father hugged you as a child and you knew that everything was going to be all right. The holding of a newborn child in your hands for the first time. Not falling, but uncontrollable crashing into new love, the un-explainable holding of hands or the first time you heard the eerie and haunting sounds of the Northern Lights.

Now imagine, if you can, no awareness of your surrounding at all. None. It is as if you were not there. There are no sounds, feelings, sights, tastes: Nothing. Replaced all with just the raw emotions felt during those times. Not just the memory of these events but the emotions themselves. In that special, magical and mystical part of your mind where emotions are stored, kept secret, safe and secure. Go to that special place, and you will know where these words come from. And yes, I do miss them so. But it is not a place I can go to by will. Some other must take me there.

Acknowledgements

Who do you thank for the life you have lived? I have to thank all of them. To those that I have loved and have loved me. To the ones I have hurt and been hurt by. Even to those I hated and those who have hated me. To my experiences: the good times, the bad times, and, of course, the ugly — Vietnam. To the Marine Corps, for teaching me some valuable life's lessons. To the Air Force, for allowing me to fly their airplanes. You start thanking, and you can't thank everyone. To my Muse who has been by my side helping me to express myself. To my shrink, Doctor "Ruby." I hope she can soon realize the very special gift she holds: Empathy. She was my Guardian Angel for a very short while, and I do miss her so. But a very special thanks to my wife of forty-one years, who has put up with all of my adventures during that time. My two beautiful and wonderful children who have given me great happiness and joy in my life and more. To my two editors, Betsy and Rachel, who helped to make the book look pretty and fixed most of the technical issues and errors. To my illustrator, Linda, who drew exactly what I asked her to draw. I hope she enjoyed the bottle of wine. And to Kelsey from "Kelsey Lynne Photography" who brought back to life pictures, some forty-seven years old, and helped design the book cover. I hope she enjoys her coffee card. I thank them all, because they have given my life richness — more richness, perhaps, than I deserve. But I'll take it anyway.

Todd M. Howe

ALL I REALLY NEED TO KNOW I LEARNED IN KINDERGARTEN
By Robert Fulghum
"Most of what I really need
to know about how to live
and what to do and how to be
I learned in kindergarten.
Wisdom was not at the top
of the graduate school mountain,
but there in the sand pile at Sunday school.
These are the things I learned:
Share everything.
Play fair.
Don't hit people.
Put things back where you found them.
Clean up your own mess.
Don't take things that aren't yours.
Say you're sorry when you hurt somebody.
Wash your hands before you eat.
Flush.
Warm cookies and cold milk are good for you.
Live a balanced life
Learn some and think some
and draw and paint and sing and dance
and play and work every day some.
Take a nap every afternoon.
When you go out into the world,
Watch out for traffic,
Hold hands and stick together.
Be aware of wonder."

The Marine Corps added and instilled in me the following: Give one hundred percent all the time, always finish what you start, and don't ever give up. If you are presented with an immovable barrier, go around it. If you cannot go around it, go over it. If the first two options don't work, then go through the *damn* thing.

Forward

A year has four seasons. My life is no exception. Each season has its own way, but my seasons do not last three months. To this point they have each lasted twenty-one years, almost to the day. Within each season there have been three seven year cycles of good times and bad. As I grow older, the cycles within the seasons become quieter now.

Some might think this story is fictitious at times. It is not! The story is completely accurate and true to each fact and detail. The only lies are lies of omission. Some things in life are too private and personal to share. All these are, in part, what makes my life what it is today: Blessed.

Why would I write a book? To make money? Not really. As Lao Tzu said, "He who knows he has enough is rich." I have enough, and that makes me rich. There are so many with much more material wealth than me, but more wealth is never enough to satisfy, and that makes them poor. Was my aim to be a published author? I have an ego, and that would be a boost. So, in part, yes. However, my main reason in writing is for when I am gone. I want my children to be able to pick it up, read it and hear my voice when they do. It is a book for all seasons but particularly for young people in the late spring and early summer of their lives. Hopefully, this will help them realize that dreams can and do come true, but they don't just come to you. You have to actively seek them out and work for them.

The Title
I was going to title my book "Two Wolves."

A CHEROKEE STORY
A young boy came to his Grandfather, filled with anger at
another boy who had done him an injustice.
The old Grandfather said to his grandson, "Let me tell you a
story. I too, at times, have felt a great hate for those that
have taken so much, with no sorrow for what they do. But hate
wears you down, and hate does not hurt your enemy. Hate is
like taking poison and wishing your enemy would die. I have
struggled with these feelings many times."
"It is as if there are two wolves inside me; one wolf is good and
does no harm. He lives in harmony with all around him and does
not take offence when no offence was intended. He will only
fight when it is right to do so, and in the right way.
But the other wolf, is full of anger.
The littlest thing will set him into a fit of temper."
"He fights everyone, all the time, for no reason. He cannot
think because his anger and hate are so great. It is helpless
anger, because his anger will change nothing. Sometimes it is
hard to live with these two wolves inside me, because both of
the wolves try to dominate my spirit."
The boy looked intently into his Grandfather's eyes and asked,
"Which wolf will win, Grandfather?"
The Grandfather smiled and said, "The one you feed."
Author Unknown

I have struggled my entire life with the evil wolf.

The title of the book comes from being around pilots most of my life. Whenever
two or more pilots get together and start talking, the conversation seems to always center around flying. Most pilot stories begin with, "There I was…" Most

of the stories are true to a point. Usually, getting better with time and memories. But almost always, containing exciting tales of near crashes and other mishaps. They should all end with, "…and here I am." But they seldom do, because the teller is telling the story. This is my story.

"*There I was…*

Spring

In Spring, there is one snowflake high in the mountains – frozen. It will begin to melt. It will join with other snowflakes, and together they will form a creek, followed by a stream. In their time, they will become a river.

Those Things That Mold Us

I was not going to write about the early years. They were not pleasant for me. I was going to start the story later, when I joined the Marines. Those things I would like to forget, I remember still, and the story wouldn't be complete without them.

My parents were both low functioning alcoholics. They were working class poor – children of the Great Depression – which haunted them for the rest of their lives. We always had a roof over our heads and food in our bellies. I thank them for that. But the Soul Food craze of the 70's didn't interest me at all. I had eaten that kind of food a lot in my life. We didn't have a lot of money, and we were thought of as poor. My mother would say, "We can't afford it," and she was right. I learned at an early age what it was like to be without money and decided someday I would have some. Being thought of as poor was unacceptable to me. So, I adopted the persona of being "cheap", because being cheap was something I had control over, unlike being poor which I did not. Unfortunately, that persona would follow me in life.

We had a single, bare light bulb in our kitchen – no fixture. It didn't have a wall switch, but a chain with a long, cotton string attached. At the end of the string was a large black button from an old Navy watch jacket with an anchor engraved on it. My parents normally had a 60-watt bulb there. One day my father came home with a 75-watt bulb, and it lit up the room. My parents then noticed the electric bill had gone up a few cents. When the 75-watt bulb burned out, they replaced it with a 40-watt bulb to recoup their losses.

One day, a group from our local church showed up at the front door with a turkey and all the fixings for Thanksgiving Dinner. I don't think I ever saw my father angrier and more hurt. We might not have had much, but he did have pride. I learned that from him that day. Oh, we didn't take the food.

Both my parents lived to be 84, dying eight years apart. They both smoked a pack of unfiltered cigarettes and consumed at least a six-pack of beer each and every day of their adult lives. Everything they cooked was fried. They had a bowl next to the stove. Each morning, they would cook up some real bacon and pour the bacon grease into that bowl. For dinner that night, they would scoop up a large quantity of the bacon grease and fry whatever we had to eat. Food had something different in those days – taste and flavor. Oh my, how good that food tasted. It was not the healthiest of diets.

They didn't work out or go to the gym, but they taught me well. I don't drink, smoke or do drugs. I work out at the gym three times per week. Bacon grease is not so much a part of my diet now. I figure if they can make it to 84, I should be able to. Anything after that, and I'll be into the bonus rounds.

The Evil Wolf

The first eighteen years of my spring were written almost solely from the evil wolf. I was angry, bitter, and hateful. During those years, the good wolf almost died.

I was born in the year 1948 as part of what was to be known as the "Baby Boom Generation." The first memory I have is of me laying in a crib. I noticed things around me. I looked at my right hand, and it moved. Then, I asked it to close and then open. Much to my surprise and delight, it did. That lesson would last a lifetime. I had control of my hand and me.

I was born with a minor birth defect. My tongue was tied to the bottom of my mouth. It made me talk funny, and children are seldom tolerant of things that are different. I was constantly teased and ridiculed. I learned to fight – and lose – early in life.

In first grade, I was in another fight, and the teacher kept me and the other kid after school. The kid beside me hit me, and I hit him back. Just like in football, the referee seldom sees the first foul but always the second. She sent an uncomplimentary note home with me to be signed by my parents and returned the next day.

My parents put me in a chair, and while blowing smoke in my face, told me to tell them the truth. So, I did, and they didn't believe me. Over and over this went on, and I thought to myself, "All I have to do is tell them what they want to hear, and they'll let me go." A few times, I considered it, and then principle intervened. I said, "Okay, I'll tell you truth. The kid hit me first, and I hit him back." I repeated it over and over again. That was a character-building moment in my life. I had principles, and no matter how unpleasant, I would not compromise them. Unfortunately, it also taught me that telling the truth didn't matter if no one believes you. The teacher wrote in my assessment: "DOES NOT PLAY WELL WITH OTHERS."

My grandfather, an old farmer, used to wear overalls all the time. I thought the world of him. When I was younger, I called him "Bucky," because when he was sitting, he would let me ride on his foot, and he would buck me up and down. My aunt thought it disrespectful and taught me to say, "Grandfather." He came over to the house one day. My aunt was there, and I called him "Grandfather." He was hurt, and I never rode on his foot again.

He gave me a pair of Little Man overalls, and I wore them to school. The kids laughed and called me names like "farmer boy." One kid put dirt down the side of my overalls. (And *I* didn't play well with others?) With that, the fight was on. The teacher broke it up and asked me why I was fighting all the time. I said, "It's because they tease me about the way I talk, and they were making fun of my overalls." She said – and I quote – "Then why don't you speak more clearly." I told her about my speech impediment. She would have nothing to do with it. She then said, "Well, maybe if you wore clothes like everyone else they wouldn't tease you." Lesson learned. As long as I conformed to the collective, everyone else, things would be okay. I was only six years old, but I knew that was bullshit. Perhaps that is where I formed my first anti-social and anti-socialist ideals.

"Anti-social behavior is a trait of intelligence in a world full of conformists" ~ *Nikola Tesla*

When I was seven I had my tonsils and adenoids removed. At the same time, they clipped the tie and freed my tongue. My tongue, once held down, was now free to bounce around the inside of my mouth. I found that my speech up to that point sounded funny, but now, I couldn't talk at all. The words wouldn't form in my mouth, and at age seven, I had to learn how to talk all over again. My parents constantly reminded me to pronounce and enunciate my words and to stop chewing my tongue. The school put me into speech therapy classes for the next three years. I thank them for that.

In the second grade, those in the education field decided they would try a new form of teaching students how to read. It was called "sight reading," and they were *excited* about the new way. Over the years, I learned to hate it when teachers said they were excited about a new program. What it means is they are going to try something new on you or your child. If it doesn't work out, they'll just go on to something else that seemed *exciting*. I was a victim of the "Dick and Jane" reading series. It taught that if you look at a word long enough, you will remember it. It didn't work for me.

At the end of the third grade, I couldn't read and was labeled a slow learner. I was being tutored by a student teacher one day. She showed me the word "THERE" and asked me to find the little word inside the big word. I looked and finally found the word "He", to which she responded, "Well, yes. That is *a* small word inside the big word, but it's not the small word we're looking for. We're looking for the word 'The' " I thought for a moment and then asked, "How am I supposed to know which little word to look for?" She responded, "If you look at them long enough, they will just pop out at you." There wasn't a whole lot of popping going on for me. By the way, the word "THERE" has the following small words inside of it: the, he, her, here and ere. And *I* was the slow learner?

Beginning in the fourth grade, I was taken out of normal class, once a week, and placed in "Remedial Reading" for an hour. (*No* stigma attached there). The purpose of the class was to remediate my deficiencies. What was remedial reading? It was phonics, the same way my sister had learned to read two years earlier, before it had become "Remedial."

I was in remedial reading for three years. By the end of the sixth grade, I was reading at a seventh grade level. I had caught up and then some. I would find throughout my life that I often started out behind, then caught up and moved ahead.

I almost left this part out, (Freudian, I think). In fourth grade, they found I had a beautiful singing voice. "Like a bird," they said — even with my speech problem, which was, by then, beginning to clear up. The problem was that I sang first soprano. No young male wants to be there. When my voice changed years later in life, it was still higher than some.

In the fifth grade, they began something called "tracking." Students were divided into three groups: A, B and C. Group A was for the really smart kids, Group B for the normal kids, and Group C for the "slow learners." I found out you didn't work as hard being in Group C. I was lazy, so that worked out for me.

A precognition (premonition). My father was on and off the wagon most of my childhood. He would normally stop drinking for a couple of weeks and then fall off the wagon and continue. When he wasn't drinking he was a pleasant human being. When he was drinking he was a sloppy, mean and obnoxious asshole. A real Dr. Jekyll and Mr. Hyde.

Note: "*The original phrase 'On the water wagon' means one has stopped drinking alcoholic beverages. A water wagon was a common piece of equipment in the days before paved roads. They were used to spray the dirt roads to help control dust. Falling 'off the wagon' would indicate a return to boozing.*" ~ *McGruff.*

He had not been drinking for about four months and I thought, finally the nightmare is over. He's made it. Life fell into a pattern of calm with peace. It had been seven months now and he still wasn't drinking.

I had a terrible dream one morning. I woke up in a panic, sweating, totally stressed out. I was on the verge of tears. I dreamt my father had fallen off of the wagon again. Then I realized I was awake and thought to myself, no it's okay he's not drinking anymore, it's all right, and it was just a bad dream that's all, just a terrible dream.

I was eleven and trotted off to school that day. When I returned home around four in the afternoon, there were both my mother and father dead drunk around the kitchen table. You have to understand most children of alcoholics blame themselves for their parent's drinking condition. Especially if those parents have told you that their lives were fine until you came along. Well there it was, less than twelve hours after the dream. What else was I supposed to think?

In the seventh grade, I became really good at adding, subtracting, multiplying and dividing numbers in my head. The teacher would call out a series of numbers and tell you to add, subtract, multiply or divide them. Sometimes, he would call twenty to thirty numbers at a time. Students were expected to do it all in their heads and come up with the answer quickly. I was competing with another student for top honors. I won and was then moved to special Group B+ in mathematics.

My eighth grade teacher recommended I take Algebra during my first year in high school. We hadn't had any Algebra in grade school. I was put in Algebra 1. Although I did math in my head quickly and correctly, I just didn't understand Algebra. I passed with a D, and the teacher told me not to take Algebra 2. I would later run into the same teacher at Portland Community College. I took his course titled, "Computer Math and Logic," and loved it. I earned an A. I don't know if he remembered me or not.

In eighth grade, the teacher talked about areas in which we might find employment in the coming years. She said, "The commercial airline business would be hot." I told her, "I could become an airline pilot," to which she replied, "Not just flying the planes, but building them, making reservations, ticketing, and all other aspects of the business." In other words: *Howe, give it up.*

I remember how throughout my childhood, when I heard an airplane flying overhead, I would run outside and count the numbers. The numbers were how many engines it had. Then, I started seeing jets, and I recognized they made a different sound.

"You can always tell when a man has lost his soul to flying. The poor bastard is hopelessly committed to stopping whatever he is doing long enough to look up and make sure the aircraft purring overhead continues on course and does not suddenly fall out of the sky. It is also his bound duty to watch every aircraft within view take off and land." ~ *Ernest K. Gann, 'Fate is the Hunter'*

Mid-way between the eighth grade and my freshman year in high school, my mother became really ill with a persistent cough. She went to the doctor numerous times. The doctor prescribed some cough syrup and some antibiotics. But she wasn't getting any better. About two months later she started coughing up blood. She returned to the doctor and the diagnosis was Tuberculosis (TB). After unsuccessful attempts to treat it on an out-patient basis, the county health board committed her to a sanitarium for tuberculosis. The parents of all my friends told them they couldn't visit me anymore because, "Only dirty people get TB."

"Tuberculosis is an infection caused by slow-growing bacteria that grow best in areas of the body that have lots of blood and oxygen. That's why it is most often found in the lungs." ~ *WebMD*

That left my father, my sister and me at home. About a month later my sister tested positive on a TB tine test, showing she had been exposed to TB. The health board decided to put my sister in the sanitarium with my mother and get her away from my father for, "Just-in-case." My father was a lot of things, but he was not a pervert. Still, the county removed her. Mom was in the sanitarium for eight months, my sister for seven.

Now it was just my father and me. He continued to drink and since his wife wasn't around to fight with, by default, I became the only one available. We lived together in a war-zone for the next seven months.

I had one pair of blue jeans my freshman year in high school. I ripped the right knee and told my father I needed another pair. At first he refused. I told him I couldn't go to school with only one pair because everyone would know I was too poor to have another pair. If he didn't get me a new pair of jeans, I told him I would stop going to school. He reluctantly agreed. Blue jeans in those days were four dollars and twenty-five cents a pair. It was a large expense in 1963. About forty dollars in today's dollars.

Finally, my mother had surgery. The surgeons removed one and one-half lobes of her lungs. There are normally five lobes, so she was down to three and one-half. In spite of this radical surgery my mother continued to smoke until she died at age 84 from Chronic Obstructive Pulmonary Disease (COPD).

Once she returned home I thought things might be better. They were not. Prior to her illness my parents had remodeled the living room and gone into debt. They replaced the old windows in the living room with two large picture glass panes. My mother loved her new windows and would look out from them often. But when she returned home from the sanitarium she closed the drapes, turned out the lights and went into seclusion. She was embarrassed, ashamed and humiliated. She lived like that for almost two years.

My friends still couldn't visit until about mid-way through my junior year. TB is just a bacterial infection, like any other. Not just, "dirty" people get it. Try and explain that to someone who is ignorant and scared. I probably would have done the same thing if it were my children.

In my senior year of high school, I was taking an English class that was even too easy for me. I was getting straight A's, so they wanted to put me in a higher level class. Too much work, I thought. I almost didn't graduate that year. I got a failing notice in a class four weeks before the end of the term — a class I needed. I worked a little harder and got a D and a diploma. I graduated with a 2.00 GPA.

High School Graduation 1966

A Love Is Born

In grade school and high school, I watched way too much television. KPTV Channel 12 in Portland, Oregon would sign off at the end of the broadcast day with the following:

High Flight
by John Gillespie Magee, Jr.
"Oh, I have slipped the surly bonds of earth,
and danced the skies on laughter-silvered wings;
Sunward I've climbed and joined the tumbling mirth of sun-split clouds –
and done a hundred things you have not dreamed of –
wheeled and soared and swung high in the sunlit silence.
Hovering there I've chased the shouting wind along
and flung my eager craft through footless halls of air.
Up, up the long delirious burning blue
I've topped the wind-swept heights with easy grace,
where never lark, or even eagle, flew;
and, while with silent, lifting mind I've trod
the high untrespassed sanctity of space,
put out my hand and touched the face of God."

Note: John Gillespie Magee, was an American pilot with the Royal Canadian Air Force in the Second World War. He came to Britain, flew in a Spitfire squadron, and was killed at the age of nineteen on 11 December 1941. This during a training flight from the airfield near Scopwick.

There was a video of a fighter plane in flight, taken by a chase aircraft. As music played in the background, those words were spoken. I had the dream of flying my whole life, but in those days, my dreams just didn't come true.

After high school, I started at a community college, which lasted all of two weeks. They wanted me to study, read the materials, write papers and other things. My counselor told me if I dropped out I would never come back to school. I would prove him wrong, many times over.

I had a part-time job, a full-time girlfriend and lost my virginity that year. It was my first, but not my last, '*Summer of 42*' (the title of a coming of age book and movie). I would be fortunate enough to have two of these experiences in my life.

Roll Over

I was driving in my 1959 Austin Healey Sprite convertible. It was a warm summer night. I drove along a stretch of road by the river, and the night cooled. With the top down and my hair blowing in the wind, I had not a care in the world. Listening to the sweet sound of the motor and the meshing of the gearbox, I asked myself, "Does it get any better than this?" I would discover later in life: Yes, it does. A lot better.

Later that summer, Mike, a friend, and I were camping and hunting up in the high country. There were a number of dirt logging roads there. The day we got there, I put the top down on the Sprite, and we went and had fun playing *Racecar Driver* in the dirt. Nice slides and everything. That night, it rained a bit and the roads now were a little wet and more slippery than greased owl shit. We went out playing again that morning. As I started to make a turn, the car continued to go straight. I was trying to control it but could not. I saw an old, rotten stump in front of me and thought, "Oh no, I'm going to hit that stump." Then, my thought changed to, "Oh no, I am going through the stump." As we blew through it, I thought, "Oh no, the car is going to roll," and it did. One three-hundred-and-sixty-degree roll. Then, I thought to myself, "Oh God, *I* could die." At that very moment, a hand reached down and grabbed me by the nape of my neck and pulled me from the car. I rolled and then landed on about four-to-six inches of moss – a very soft landing. I lay with my hands and feet down, looking up the hill, without a scratch on me. Mike didn't fare as well. He was pretty beaten up. I saw the Sprite, damaged and sitting upside-down on a stump. Yes, it had made another one-hundred-and-eighty-degree roll. There were about four inches of clearance between the top of my seat and the top of the stump. I would have been compressed in that area if I been wearing a seat belt. My Guardian Angel's first, but certainly not last, intervention.

Time to Get On With My Life

This is where the book was going to begin.

I wanted to join the Marines. It seemed a good idea at the time – the Vietnam War and all. I had to take a battery of tests. I must have paid some attention in class somewhere along the line, because this *slow learner* did extremely well on all of his tests. Perhaps, I had applied myself.

I didn't really come to life until March of 1967, the day I entered the Unites States Marine Corps. It was cold, wet and quite blustery in Portland, Oregon that day. My parents and girlfriend had come out to the airport to see me off. I hadn't gotten any sleep the night before and was nervously awaiting what was ahead. At the airport, someone opened a door to the outside tarmac. A gust of wind blew in a moist, delicious smell. At that moment, it was permanently etched into my sinuses and memory. It was the smell of burnt jet fuel on a cold morning. *Damn*, that smelled good. I thought to myself, "I could live with that smell around me for the rest of my life."

We said our farewells, and then I boarded a big old jet airliner: a Boeing 707. I found out later we had gone to a different runway that day, one normally used in inclement weather. The pilot positioned us at the end of that runway. Then, with the breaks full-on, he ran the engines up to full take-off power. I found out later that this was called a "static takeoff." He then jumped off the breaks. There was nothing smooth about it, and we were pushed firmly back into our seats. I thought, "That was kind of cool."

As we began to roll down the runway, I thought, "No… This is *way* cool." The aircraft swayed from left to right, the wind buffeting its sides as the pilot fought to keep it on the centerline. I looked at the overhead bins and noticed they were swaying back and forth. There were sounds and movements I had never experienced before, and then we started to lift into the air. I felt a buzz go through my body – a tingle in my ass and stomach. I said to myself, "I have got to have more of this." Like a drug addict, I just wanted more. I was addicted.

The flight from PDX (Portland) to SFO (San Francisco) went by too quickly. Too soon, we were landing, and I felt that buzzing sensation again. Later in life, I would feel it every time I took off and landed in an airplane.

We deplaned and started waiting. One of the new Marines had been put in charge and was already getting into his role, yelling and carrying on. Too funny. We waited a very long time for the next airplane. It was a smaller jet, maybe a B-727. We flew from SFO to LGB (Long Beach). We landed and waited again until well into the evening. Did I mention we hadn't had anything to eat all day? I had brought some beef jerky with me because I had heard stories of no food, no sleep, and the yelling, but for all my preparation, nothing could have equipped me for what was ahead. They put us on an even smaller prop plane, and we flew from LGB to SAN (San Diego). We landed a little after midnight — no food nor sleep all day.

It was there that we met our first drill instructor. He lined us up on the sidewalk outside the terminal and started yelling all kinds of obscenities at us. Civilians were walking by, trying to avert their eyes and cover their ears. As all this was going on, I noticed a Navy bus picking up their recruits. Their driver / drill instructor and recruits were standing around shooting the shit — smoking and laughing. At that moment, I thought to myself, "Uh oh. Did I make a mistake?"

Finally, after about an hour of standing at rigid attention, a pick-up truck — not a bus — with a cover over the bed and USMC markings on its side showed up at the curb. There were about twenty of us: some from Portland, others from all around the states, and later we would find, from all over the world. They crammed all twenty of us into the back of that pick-up, and away we went.

The truck ride was uncomfortable. I think we hit every rock, bump and pothole in the road. Turns were not particularly smooth. Finally, we came to the gate, and the guards let us in. Getting out, I found, would be much harder than getting in. Suddenly, the truck came to an abrupt stop. I then heard yelling from numerous voices in every direction, "Get off of the truck! Get off the truck, and get on the yellow foot prints!" I had no idea what or where the yellow foot prints were. At this point, all I wanted to do was get out of the back of the truck. There on the asphalt were painted, yellow footprints — all in formation and pointing towards a large wall. There on the wall, written in Marine Corps colors, scarlet and gold, were a number of infractions that could get you thrown into the brig, Marine Corps jail. A drill instructor was now reading them out to us. I don't think they knew how to talk at a normal volume, because they never did. It was always shouting, and they acted very strangely indeed.

We were marched into a barber shop with multiple mind games to follow. There was a young Marine in front of me, and after he was moved through the process, it was my turn. I looked at myself in a mirror with all my hair and civilian clothes. They sat me down in the barber chair. There was no option for "a little off the sides, and leave the top." Nope. Instead, the whole haircut took about fifteen seconds, and I was then directed to the next station. The whole time, we were in lines. The next mirror I saw revealed my hairless head. The transition had begun. We spent the remainder of the night and early morning having all our gear issued to us. We were instructed on how to take a shower, shave, etc. As the sun was coming up, we were carrying our gear to our Quonset huts. The Marines love their Quonset huts, as I would find out later. I spent a lot of time in them and learned to call them "home." We were instructed on how to make a bed, even though we wouldn't have an opportunity to use one for a while. We were marched over to the Chow Hall and given about two minutes to consume a meal of runny eggs and other goodies. The remainder of the day was spent learning how to become a Marine.

*Note: When I joined the Marines, I was six-feet tall and weighed one-hundred-and-seventeen pounds. The Corps put me on the "Thin Man" program. A drill instructor would follow me through the Chow Line and tell the server to give me extra portions. However, I wasn't given any additional time to eat them. The Marines had a poster on the wall in the Chow Hall which read, "**TAKE ALL YOU WANT, BUT EAT ALL YOU TAKE.**" It was a challenge for me to eat it all.*

That night, we finally got to sleep. They wouldn't let us have watches, so we didn't know what time it was. I do know it was very late. We finally got some sleep — about two or three hours. This, after being awake for about sixty hours. I found out later that I could do sixty-hour days over and again.

Morning came way too early. We awoke to the sounds of garbage can lids being thrown down the center of our Quonset hut. The drill instructors were again making loud, almost unintelligible sounds — with barely enough clarity to understand them. That was Day Three. They then started testing us to see what jobs we might be suitable for and how we might best be useful for, "The needs of the Marine Corps." The Marines had historically scored lower on these tests than other branches of the military services. In later years, the Marines began testing earlier and saved the indoctrination phase until later in the program.

The remainder of our nine weeks there, shortened from the norm of thirteen, was due to the, "Needs of the Marine Corps." Translation: They had to replace all the Marines who were being killed and wounded in Vietnam. They had such a way with words. The rest of the training was and is kind of a blur. We went to the rifle range, learned how to shoot, march, drill, eat and other things millions of Marines before us had done. I learned a valuable life lesson there that has served me well for the remainder of my life: Marines finish what they start. There is no quitting. You just put one foot in front of the other, and then you are there. It makes no difference how tired or weary you are, you just do. Task Completion, I call it.

"The journey of a thousand miles begins with a single step." - Lao Tzu.

I'm going to School! Or Am I?

I was interviewed during Boot Camp about what I might do in the Corps. I did well on the sleep deprivation test. They found out I could do some typing and gave me a test. I was going to flunk typing in high school before I dropped the class. This, before my ideals of Task Completion. I had enough memory of it to actually pass the Marine Corps' basic typing skills test. Upon graduation, I was told I would be going to school to learn how to become a Communication/ Message Center and Teletype Operator. I was going to school.

The next phase of our training was ITR (Infantry Training Regimen). We traveled north by bus from San Diego to Camp Pendleton, California. When we got off the bus, there were our drill instructors. They had arrived there before us in cars and were waiting. I thought, "Oh crap…They're going to join us," but they didn't. They just wanted to mess with our minds one last time. They were successful.

During ITR, one of the instructors actually went human on us one day. He told us what our lives were going to be like from now on. He said, "All your old friends from high school will drift away. They won't know you anymore. All that was is no more. Your girlfriends will send you Dear John letters, and you're never going to be the same again." At the time, I thought he was full of shit, but he was so right. His words would came back to haunt me for years after that.

My training at ITR was to be that of a "POG" (Personnel Other than Grunt). It was a shortened version of the normal course – only three-and-a-half weeks long. About two weeks into the training, I was beginning to see the light at the end of the tunnel. Then, I realized it might be an oncoming train. The Marines got cut up pretty badly in Vietnam. I think it was called "Hill 881." They lost a lot of good, young Marines there – boys too young to complete this journey we call, "Life."

There were about two-hundred-and-twenty of us in the POG Training Company. After Hill 881, the "Needs of the Marine Corps" changed. Shortly thereafter, in morning formation, about sixty names were called out, and they were sent to the long ITR course. They were going to become Basic Infantry, 0311 MOS (Military Occupational Specialty). The next day, about forty more names were called. They too were gone. On the third day, twenty-one names were called. Mine was the last name they called that day. Then, they said, "No, Howe, get back into the formation. You're on tomorrow's list." That night, I didn't get much sleep. The next morning during formation, they didn't call my name. Nor were there any names called for the remainder of the training. My Guardian Angel again.

At the completion of my ITR, I finally got home on some leave. I flew home and back, getting that same feeling every time the plane took off and landed. *Wow! What a rush!*

When I got home, I couldn't believe how everyone *else* had changed. I went to visit my old boss and friend, Sig. He was Jewish and from the *old country*. He had never married and had no children. We developed a very father-and-son type of relationship. He was so very proud of me and would be even more so in years to come. He would later say, "I always knew there was greatness in you, even if you didn't know it yourself."

The time on leave went by quickly, too quickly, and my girlfriend and first love seemed more distant than I remembered. After I got back from my leave, she sent me a "Dear John" letter. Welcome to the Marine Corps.

Why Not A Hundred Percent?

I entered Communications School. It was at the same base that boot camp had been – just on a different part of the base. We could see the recruits going through their marching drills and physical training. It had only been a few months before, but it seemed like a lifetime had passed.

We entered the training program. It was a little more lax than ITR but not much. We were still Marines after all. I wasn't much of student in high school. (Remember, I graduated with a 2.00 GPA). That was only because I took the easy classes. I didn't read the materials or write the papers or study for the tests. I found later that if you do all these things you score much better. Better grades now became important to me. I wanted to complete the class successfully and not have the "Needs of the Marine Corps" change my MOS.

I was studying and had an eighty-three percent average. Then, one day one of the instructors took a personal interest in me. I thank him for that. He called me aside and gave me a memorable ass-chewing. He said, "You're more intelligent and better than your grades would indicate. You're not trying hard enough, *Marine*." I replied, "I have an eighty-three percent average." (Which I thought was pretty good, after high school and all). He looked me straight in the eye and said, "Why not a hundred percent, *Marine*?" At first I thought, "*Bull Shit*. A hundred percent? That's crazy." I thought him a fool, but then I asked myself, "Why *not* a hundred percent?" That simple talk changed my life forever. I am sure my children wished I had never heard it. I asked the same of them many times over in the years to follow.

The class had a number of written tests and a lot of practical tests. I was the first Marine ever to score a hundred percent on one of the tests that had over three-hundred-and-thirty parts. The parts had to be in the correct order and sequence. My mentor took me aside afterwards and said, "I told you, you could do it, Marine, and you did." I found I was smarter than my records would indicate, and for the remainder of my life, I always asked myself, "Why *not* a Hundred Percent?"

The school was about two-months long, and then we graduated. I was toward the top of the class — not number one, because of that eighty-three percent thing at the beginning — but my attitude, ambition and self-confidence had changed forever. *Task Completion. Never quit. Why not* a hundred percent? These had become the rules to live by. I would no longer settle for just "good enough." At the completion of training, we were all given orders to Okinawa for further transfer to FMFPAC (Fleet Marine Force, Pacific), Ground Forces. We were all going to Vietnam.

Before I left for the Pacific, I returned home for a short leave. Life never was the same. At this point, leave seemed both too short and too long. I actually wanted to get back to the Corps. It was beginning to become my home.

Once again, I flew from PDX to SFO. I picked up some ground transportation to Travis Air Force Base, awaiting civilian charter to Okinawa. I noticed a much more relaxed attitude with the Air Force than with the Marine Corps — even in the way they carried themselves. Parts of me wished I was where they were, others not. The conflict between wanting a laxer lifestyle and the strict discipline of the Marines would be resolved in the years to come.

We boarded a very large aircraft and flew from SFO to ANC (Anchorage, Alaska). I found out later that with our load, fuel, headwinds, etc., we wouldn't have been able to make it all the way without a stop. They let us out at a hangar away from the civilians to keep us from intermingling with "real people" and for fear that we might go AWOL (absent without leave). It took a couple of hours for them to refuel, restock food and water, and clean the biffies. Then, on we went. We landed in Okinawa at night. They had transportation waiting for us and hustled us off to the Marine Corps Base, Camp Butler. From there, it was a continual series of *hurry up* and *wait*. We had to put all of our stateside gear and uniforms in storage. We wouldn't be needing them. We were given a four-hour familiarization course on the M-16. Not enough, really. Finally, we were ready to go to Vietnam.

Going To Vietnam

There were three of us who had gone to Communications School together. We all had the same MOS – 2542. We were lined up waiting to find out where we would be sent. I was number two in line. I didn't have enough copies of my orders. So, I got out of line, grabbed more copies from my sea bag and returned. Pappy, a name given to him because he was a couple of years older than the rest of us, took my place in line and gave me a look like, *You left it, and now it's mine.* I didn't argue with him, because he was right. I had gotten out of line and given up my spot in doing so. The orders came down. Numbers one and two were going to 2nd Battalion, 5th Marines. I was going by myself to 1st Battalion, 7th Marines. I wanted to be with someone I knew. I asked Pappy if he wanted to change with me. He said, "No." Besides, the Marines had already drawn up the orders, and the Marines don't make mistakes. That way, they never have to change anything. My two friends and classmates went north to a place named Khe Sanh, which saw some of the bloodiest and longest fighting of the Vietnam War. They were under siege from January 21st to June 9th, 1968. I was sent to Hill 10, west of Da Nang. My war was shorter and less intense than theirs. I saw Pappy in July or August of that year. His unit had come to Hill 10 to regroup. He reminded me that it should have been me that went to Khe Sanh and that where I had been wasn't the "real" war. I reminded him that it was his choice to take my spot in line. He only kind of cringed. My Guardian Angel again.

We Won the Toss and Elected to Receive

Welcome to Vietnam. I arrived in country in November 1967 and was assigned to 1/7/1, Hill 10, West of Da Nang, RVN (Republic of Vietnam). I was just nineteen-years-old. We could see Laos from our hill. It was quiet for all of November. Then, in December and January, we started to pick up harassing mortar fire at night. It was a good thing. It got our attention and helped us to prepare for what was coming. Was I in combat? I was not in the bush. Our hill was a battalion firebase with 105 Howitzers and 81mm mortars. During Tet 1968, I think everyone was in combat. I know I certainly was.

I was working the twelve-hour dayshift. I was in my hooch, in my bunk, fully-dressed but without my boots on. It was night and very dark. I heard the mortars coming out of their tubes off in the distance and knew they were incoming. The guy across the hooch started yelling, "Incoming! Incoming!" I had my boots on untied, flak jacket, cartage belt, helmet on my head, and was out the hatch (doorway) in maybe three to five seconds. By the time I got to the hatch, the shit was hitting the fan big time. It was five steps to the ground, and I took one. There was a four-man bunker outside the hooch to the right that I bypassed. We were supposed to marshal at the Communications Bunker after any attack. I went there first. Don't know why really, but I just did. There were mortars dropping all over the hill everywhere. They fell like rain. Then, I heard my first incoming 122mm Katyusha Rocket. It did not sound like a freight train. It sounded like what it is, a 122mm rocket. Nothing else in the world makes that sound incoming. It does not go boom. It goes *crack*.

I was hot-footing it to the Communications Compound and bunker. There had been a roll of concertina wire around the compound. I was jumping it one day, I had been pretty good at track in high school. The Captain saw what I was doing and added a second roll of wire for security. It was a good call on the Captain's part, but for me to get to the entrance to the compound now, it was about thirty yards out of my way, and I was in a hurry. *Ya think?* It was also ninety-degrees to my route of travel (the shortest distance between two points being a straight line). The only thing between me and the perceived safety of the bunker were two rows of concertina wire. I jumped and made it three-quarters of the way over. My cartage belt was buckled and over my left arm. My left hand was on my helmet and my right hand held my M-16. The wire caught my right shin and tumbled me to the ground. My boots were still untied, and to this day, I think I could have made the jump if they had been tied. Anyway, I did a three-hundred and sixty-degree roll on the ground, head over heels, and came up running – didn't miss a step.

I stormed into the Communications Bunker. It was a bunker of about twenty-feet by forty-feet. Half was open bay, and the other half had the switch board and message center, where I worked. The open area now started to fill with the wounded. A Navy Corpsman – *God bless them all* – said, "Let me take care of that." I looked around and then realized he was talking to me and was pointing to my right leg. It was dirty and bleeding, pretty badly – *concertina wire will do that to you* – and my Cami's (jungle utilities) were all torn up. He laid me down on a stretcher and cut them up to my crotch. I remember that, because it was the only pair of jungle utilities I had. All the rest were stateside. Supply was out of the Cami's (Jungle Utilities). I thought, *why couldn't it have been the stateside ones?* Funny, what goes through your mind when you are close to death. Anyway, he cleaned up my leg and put a battle dressing on it. Then, he tried to get my service information to put me in for a Purple Heart Medal. I refused to give it to him, because I had done it to myself. I got up and felt like crap, because some of the Marines coming in were really effed up. I had taken the Corpsman's time and supplies for myself. The bunker became a temporary aid station.

Our hill was small, maybe three-quarters of a mile long and a couple of hundred yards across. That night they put one-hundred-and-twenty 122mm rockets on our hill, and we could not count the number of mortars. They fell like rain. There was one huge blast. I remember it well. I thought the Communications Bunker was coming down. It didn't. I had just run through that shit-storm without a scratch, other than my self-inflicted wound. The attack lasted for what seemed like forever. Actually, I think it was about fifteen or twenty minutes. After the initial barrage, our Commander was concerned that the enemy might be coming through the wire, so he ordered us all to the lines. I was told to stay behind because of my "injury," (it just kept getting worse). My Gunny Sergeant, on orders from the Captain, told me and another Marine to get on top of the Communications Bunker and guard the entrance to the Communication Compound – the same entrance I had bypassed earlier.

Note: I never knew a Gunnery Sergeant that was anything other than top notch.

There were no defensive positions on top of the bunker, and we were exposed. I remember the flares. We turned that dark night into daylight and did it all night long. There were so many flares, and my buddy and I were highlighted against the sky by the light. We started taking AK-47 fire. The bullets were just above and to the left of my ear, maybe eight inches away. Green tracers from the village were aimed at me, and it got personal. I dropped flat on the roof of the bunker. My face was flush against the fiberglass sandbags as I tried to eat my way further down. Then, my Gunny was yelling at us to get the hell off of the roof. No argument from me, Gunny. We did a low crawl over to the edge and dropped down by the entrance of the bunker. There was a wall of sandbags in front of the entrance. Gunny told us to take up our defensive positions there, guarding the entrance to the compound, the bunker, and the wounded Marines inside.

There were five dead Marines under ponchos in front of the wall. It could have been me. I remember the stench of stale urine. We checked and neither one of us had pissed ourselves. Hey, that happens. It's combat. I couldn't get the smell out of my nostrils. I didn't know where it came from or why. I stood guard there all night. The enemy took out a couple of line guard bunkers with RPG's (Rocker Propelled Grenades). There was an exchange of small arms fire along the entire perimeter line throughout most of the night.

Okay, now the following was lost to me for almost forty-three years. After fifteen months of in-depth psychoanalysis and psychotherapy, I got it to come out of me. That wire that I had, *mostly*, jumped over, was my safety. Behind it, I was safe. Outside the wire was a blur, like a fog. My shrink – I love her dearly – said that I had acted as my own therapist. I knew the wire was my safety, and I didn't want to come out from behind it. Although it was safe, it also imprisoned me. I mentally walked up to that wire many times in the following years, turned and walked away.

One day, I finally walked up and did a ninety-degree right turn toward the gate. When I got there, I could still see a fog outside, but I didn't want to go through. Then a force *pushed me through*. I didn't do it on my own. I tried to turn my head and look behind me, but I could not. It was, in fact, behind me now, and the fog had cleared. I had a recurring dream for years after the events of that night and the following day. I would wake up sweating, hot, all stressed out while trying to push something over.

I will now get to the events of the following morning. I saw what had happened that night. Everything – and I mean everything – was blown to hell: the chow hall, the hooches, the bunkers. The bunker I had bypassed coming out of the hooch had taken a direct mortar round right beside it which had collapsed the entire thing. The Marines inside were okay but were half-buried under a mound of sandbags until someone dug them out. The smell was from our urinal. A urinal in Vietnam was a pipe pounded into the ground with very large funnel attacked to it. Laugh if you will, but it was functional. Marines had been pissing into that urinal for years. It was about twenty yards from the Communications Bunker. We think it had taken a direct hit right down the funnel. It made a huge hole in the ground and scattered stale urine all over the hill. It took months for the smell to calm down. For me, the smell never went away completely. I spent time in both the Marines and the Air Force. The Air Force uses a deicing compound "Urea" on the runways. Whenever an aircraft would take off in front of us, they would heat up the fluid, and it would get into our air conditioning system and stink to high heaven. It's the same smell you get with an aircraft biffy after a long flight. I don't recall remembering Vietnam at those times. I just had an involuntary muscle contraction in my gut. Sometimes, it was just a little cringe, but sometimes, it was a lot more. We adapt. I got used to it. To this day, I am the one who cleans the bathrooms in our house. No one can clean like a Marine, and I can't stand that smell. Lynyrd Skynyrd's "That Smell" has a special meaning to me. "*Ooooh that smell. Can't you smell that smell? The smell of death surrounds you.*"

The next morning, we began feverishly filling new sandbags. We found that the fiberglass bags melt when hit with a rocket or mortar, and the canvas bags rot. We built defensive positions on top of the Communications Bunker and added two additional layers around it, for a total of five layers. After I had seen what a 122mm rocket could do, I don't think the five layers would have stopped a direct hit. Though, it might have slowed it down some. What I don't remember was having any emotions. I don't remember being afraid, even though I must have been scared shitless. I wasn't angry, sad, or anything – just totally devoid of all emotion. It was as if that part of me was gone. We were ordered to police the hill. We were to clean all debris off the road and put it on the side. If we found any unexploded ordinance, we were to mark the location, not touch it, and notify someone immediately.

There were two radio relay Marines who had built a two-man sleeping bunker where they could sleep in relative safety. It was three layers thick, with two

105mm ammo boxes, filled with dirt, on the inside and one sandbag layer cover-
ing the outside. About three feet in front of the entrance, they had built a blast
wall. It was a good design but had one fatal flaw: a canvas roof. The only way they
could get hurt would be by a direct hit from above by a mortar or if a rocket hit
them. The bunker took a direct hit with a mortar, right through the canvas roof.
The blast was contained within the walls, and not a single piece of shrapnel got
out. The blast wall in front was completely knocked over. The inside of the bunker
was burnt and bloody. Those inside had literally been blown to pieces. We finished
the road swipe and were on our way back when a Staff Sergeant (E-6) started
yelling and going all stupid on us — yelling at us to pick up the body parts. One
Marine was blown off below the waist. He was lighter than I expected for his size.
We also picked up other body parts: arms, legs, etc. The Staff Sergeant then told
us to push the bunker over and bury it. We tried, but it was built too well. We
pushed and sweated, all the while with him yelling at us, acting the fool. We were
stressed out. I hadn't had any real sleep for over a month, and the last sixteen
hours had been eventful. In addition to that, we hadn't had any chow for eighteen
hours. Finally, the Sergeant told us how effing worthless we were. He went on to
tell us to get two five-gallon cans full of diesel fuel oil and burn the bunker. We
got the fuel, started the fire, and then he told us to "get the hell out of here." As
we were walking back, I noticed there were fires all over the hill — about ten to
fifteen. So many fires. Too many.

*Note: Until my visit with the shrink and writing this, I didn't remember the bunker.
Like I said before, I don't recall any of my emotions — being mad, sad, angry, or happy
to be alive. I don't remember any of those — not even to this day. But since the memory of
that night has returned and my writing about it, I no longer have that recurring dream.*

I extended in Vietnam for an additional six months. I did so because if I had returned to the states as scheduled, I stood a good chance of returning to Vietnam
for a full year. I also felt that I hadn't done enough yet. I went home on thirty
days of additional leave as part of the deal for extending. All my friends were different. There was no longer a connection. While I was gone the entire Battalion
moved from Hill 10 to Hill 37.

There are a lot of stories I could tell about Vietnam — other life-threatening events — but one story is enough. Sometimes, it is too much.

Waiting for my flight date back to the "World"

All the "short timers" in Vietnam had a countdown calendar. When you became a "Twin Digit Midget" with ninety-nine days or less to go, you were officially a short timer. I had gone over to administration about forty-five days prior to my scheduled departure, then thirty-five, and then twenty-five to see if I had a flight date, but nothing had come down. I was beginning to wonder if I was ever going to leave Vietnam. Then, when I had *seventeen* days left, I went over to administration to ask again. The Marine, behind the desk, looked at me and said, "Are you trying to be a smartass?" I had no idea what he was talking about. I was just standing there with a big question mark on my forehead. He looked at me with contempt and then said, "I just sent a runner over to your Communications Platoon. You are leaving the hill tomorrow. You have to go to Hill 55: Regimental Headquarters today and get your medical and pay records." It was past noon, but I hustled my butt over to the Command Center as quickly as I could. I met the runner on my way, and he gave me copies of my orders. I checked in with Air-Operations to see if I could catch a chopper over to Hill 55. It was too late in the day to go by motorcade, because they're were too many snipers on the road at that time. As luck would have it, they had a Huey Helicopter coming into the LZ (Landing Zone) in about ten minutes. They put my name on the manifest. The Communications Bunker was co-located with Operations and Air Operations. The LZ was about fifty feet away from the entrance to our bunker. Sure enough, along came the chopper. I hitched a ride over to Hill 55. That was my first ride in a chopper in Vietnam.

Regiment was a lot more "shined" away than the battalion rats. We were a little more squared away than company grunts. They, being the ones who do all the real work of being Marines. Regiment gave me some shit about not being timely and not having my boots shined, but I out-processed there in record time, so I didn't give a shit about what they said or the looks I got.

I returned to Air Operations Hill 55, looking for a ride back to my Hill 37. A CH-46 helicopter was coming in about ten minutes. I got on the manifest, and shortly thereafter, I was on my way home, via Hill 37 and Da Nang. We landed on my hill in the late afternoon.

I sat on top of the Communications Bunker and a Captain came by. I got up and saluted him. He wanted to know what I was doing. I told him I had been in-country for seventeen-and-a-half months. I said. "I am going home tomorrow, and I was just saying good-bye." He actually understood, and said, "Carry on, Marine." I looked out over the fields, rice paddies and mountains. For the first time in all my time there, it was beautiful.

That night, of course, there was a party. We had to celebrate my going away, and celebrate, we did. The gomers had an appetite suppressant in liquid form. Take a tablespoon one hour before chow, and it would suppress your appetite. I had never used it before. A Marine handed the [6-8 oz.] bottle to me and said, "Here, you're going to need this tonight. Drink half the bottle." I did. That was the one and only time I ever did Speed in my entire life, and I did it somewhat inadvertently. I was up all night and couldn't stop talking. We partied until we couldn't anymore. The others wimped out on me, but I kept going. I walked over to the Communications Center and talked with them for a long while. Then, the other Marines started to get up, and I talked to them. By morning, I was almost hoarse. My OIC (Officer in Charge) talked with me and was wishing me well. I told him I couldn't get to sleep all night. He gave me a look. Officers and Senior NCO's had been briefed on this elixir called "Obese-a-tal." He asked me why I couldn't sleep. The thing about Speed is that it makes your mind work very quickly. I said, "Sir, I've been in country for seventeen-and-a-half months, and I'm going home today. I just couldn't get to sleep." He bought it. Then, I did a very stupid thing that morning. I caught the first Motor-T (transport) off the hill. If you're going to get snipped at or find an IED (Improvised Explosive Device), they normally go for the first trucks. I rode all the way into Da Nang wondering.

In Da Nang, we got off the truck and everything was confusing, of course – where to go, where to get chow, etc., but they mother-henned us pretty well. I was told my flight wasn't until the next day. I would have to spend one more night in country. I slept well that night. The next day, we formed lines and wait-ed. Then, we hurried and waited until we lined up for the freedom flight home. We boarded and buckled in. We were waiting for the mortars and rockets to come take us away before the airplane could, but we taxied out, lined up, and we were gone. You would think the aircraft would have erupted in shouts of joy and relief. It did not. I did not. It was strangely quiet, too quiet, and remained so even after we landed in Okinawa.

My war was over.

After Vietnam

I went to Okinawa and waited for air transportation to the states. The Sergeant in charge said if we did a good job cleaning the barracks and heads, we would get liberty. Liberty meant we would be able to go to town, run the whores and get some beer. The evening formation was held at 1800 hours (6 pm). The Sergeant said he had never seen the barracks, heads and everything this clean before, but the Sergeant who writes the Liberty Chits left at 1700 hours (5 pm), so he could not write the Chits today. "Maybe tomorrow" he told us. That night, another Marine and I climbed over the fence surrounding the base. We were now technically AWOL (absent without leave). We walked into town, got laid, had some beer and repeated that most of the night. We got back around 0200 hours (2 am). The next day, the Sergeant said, "If you do a real good job cleaning today, we'll issue you liberty chits." I already knew Marines weren't the smartest, but *really?* So, I didn't help clean up that day, and about thirty percent of my fellow Marines joined me. At 1800 hours, we got the same message as the day before: No Liberty Chits. That night, we jumped the fence again and walked into town. However, this time, there were seven of us. Again we availed ourselves of the local attractions and came home around 2 am. All of this was, of course, illegal, but I had been to Vietnam and wasn't about to put up with anymore bullshit. The next day was the same. Only about a third of the Marines made any effort to clean, but that night we were issued Liberty Chits. For one night out of three, I went into town legally. We had to be back that night by 2200 hours (10 pm).

When we left for Vietnam, we left behind a lot of our uniforms that we wouldn't be needing. When we got to Okinawa, the sea bags full of our gear were waiting for us. I was surprised. Now, we would have to start looking and acting like "real" Marines again. *Bullshit*. I had lived real for the last year-and-a-half.

We gathered our gear and loaded up for the long road trip to the airport, and, as it turned out, the return trip back. I made the trip to the airport three times. The rain in Okinawa is like few places I have ever seen: sideways, up and down. All three times, I got drenched and didn't seem to mind too much. On the third trip, I finally got a seat. I was on my way back home to the "real world."

The Unreal Real World

It was non-stop and a very long trip to SFO. When we arrived, they said there was a problem with some of our baggage, and they wanted to inspect it. In place of letting them paw through my things, I opened up my sea bag and dumped the entire contents — and I mean everything — out on the tarmac. The poor guy conducting the inspection was only doing his job, but I was spent. I had enough, and I just wanted to go home on some leave.

I caught another plane from SFO to PDX. I was home. I was in uniform, had read and seen the news, but I didn't expect what I came home to. I got off the plane and no one spit on me, but one young man called me a "Baby Killer." I objected to it, although in uniform, and explained to him in the only terms I knew how, my dissatisfaction with his remark. Verbally, I backed him up against a wall — yelling, screaming and going all Marine Corps Drill Instructor on him. Then, I told him I had not killed any babies and suggested that perhaps he keep his free speech to himself. Marines don't necessarily redact their expletives.

Everything had changed. Attitude, dress, mannerisms, speech. Everything, and I don't think for the better. The hippies — the ones who lost the war for us here at home — seemed to be running the show and ruining it all. They now run the country, but that's another book for another day.

I had thirty days leave, and then it was gone. I didn't fit in at home, but I also wasn't anxious to return to the Corps. I bought a used 1966 Corvette Convertible and found a girlfriend while I was home. She joined me on my trip to Twenty-nine Palms, California – the garden spot of the world and the Corps. I put her on a bus in Bakersfield, California. She didn't have enough money, so I helped her out (and dodged that bullet).

Now, I was running a little low on cash. I had no credit card and no checking account – just a little cash. No problem. I could make it to the base and then some. While driving near Barstow, California, I smelled raw gas. I pulled over to the side of the road, left the engine running and opened the hood. The fuel pump had failed and gas was shooting all over the place. I turned off the motor and took a deep breath, hoping it wouldn't go boom. Shortly thereafter, a CHP (California Highway Patrolman) came by. It would not be my last encounter with the CHP. He stopped and wanted to know what was going on, so I told him. Then, he lit up a cigarette. I asked him to refrain because of all the gas leaking out and the fumes. So, he put it out and called me a tow truck. The wrecker towed me to their repair shop. They said it would take a couple of hours to get the part and put me back on the road. It took longer, of course, but they got it fixed, and I paid them. Then, I had to use my last dollar to put in half a tank of regular. I couldn't afford Ethel (premium). It had turned dark, and the repair people warned me, "Don't go east out into the desert at night. It can be dangerous out there." I had to report by midnight and thought I didn't have a choice. So, I departed Barstow at night. I thought the best way to go would be east on I-40 to Amboy and then south on North Amboy Rd to Twenty-nine Palms. That way, I would have more time on the freeway. That decision almost cost me my life.

The Ambush

I plotted it out so I would arrive at base just before midnight and have just enough gas. East on I-40. Everything was fine until I turned toward Amboy, California. Little did I know about dry land pirates. In Amboy, they had a spotter that would radio ahead to an ambush team. The team would set up a false accident scene and wait – a pickup truck with a lost load, a mattress laying in the roadway in my lane and other debris scattered around. There was a somewhat attractive young lady waiving her arms, trying to flag me down and get me to pull over, but I was late, and it just didn't seem right. That time in Vietnam and this felt like an ambush. I remembered the words at the repair shop, so I weaved my way around the debris and put them in my rearview. About twenty miles further down the road was another spotter car. He actually blinked his lights at me when I passed. Something just wasn't right. I got to base in time and almost made it to the gas station the next day. I ran out of gas as I was pulling up to the pumps. I was literally running on fumes.

About six months or so later, the cops busted a car theft ring working out of Amboy. The pirates had spotters at both ends of the trap and radios for communication. They would spot a car they wanted and radio ahead to set the trap. When a normal motorist would see the staged accident scene, they would pull over. The pirates would then kill the motorist and bury the body in the desert — never to be found. The pirates would drive the car to Los Angeles that night, and it would be parted out by morning. That sequence of events caused a favorable outcome for me. My Guardian Angel, with me always.

Welcome to Twenty-nine Palms

I was driving up to the headquarters to check in, doing the posted speed limit of 25 mph. An MP (Military Police) just joining shift saw me driving from the other side of the parade ground, about two blocks away. We were going in the same direction. He turned on his lights and came charging at my position at about 50 mph. He pulled me over for speeding. I told him I was going the posted speed limit, so he let me go with a warning, saying, and "We know this car." That would not be the last time I heard those words.

I settled into my position at Twenty-nine Palms. I was working in an air conditioned Communications Center. This, not for the comfort of the Marines, but to keep the equipment cool. It gets hot in the desert. In the summer, no matter which shift you worked, it was never an optimal situation. If you worked nights, then you tried to get some sleep during the day. Marines are not known to be quiet. Still, it was cool in the early morning. The barracks were made of concrete, and they would heat up during the day and hold heat all night long. So if you worked days, it was bloody hot at night – too hot to sleep. Finally, in the latter part of September and beginning of October, it cooled off, and I fell in love with the desert.

70 in a 65

A fellow Marine and I decided to make a trip to Mexico. We hopped in my Corvette and across the desert we went. We ended up in Yuma, Arizona, and crossed the border to see what could be seen. We were on our way home, and it was late night, close to midnight. The moon was almost full. I don't know how many of you have seen the desert with a full moon, but it turns a black night into dusk. We were driving down a two-lane secondary road. It was dry – desert dry – and semi-light. We had the top down, and I was doing about 70 mph. The speed limit was 65 mph in those days. I saw a car up ahead and decided to pass. I pulled into the passing lane and accelerated to 80 or 90 mph. I saw a second car about a half-mile up the road and decided I would pass him too. *To the floor with the dinosaur killer!* The accelerator needle was passing 100, and I noticed a third car pull out and become the number two car in line. We were all going in the same direction, but I was in the newly-designated passing lane. So while I was out there, I thought I would just knock off the other two – make it a trifecta. As I passed the second car, doing well in excess of 120 mph, I looked over and noticed it was the CHP. *Oh, shit!*

He was close to the car in front of him – danger close. I passed him and the third car, turned on my blinker and pulled back into my lane. I relaxed my foot off the dinosaur slayer. Remember how I said the night was like dusk, semi-light? All of a sudden, it was really bright out. The CHP now pulled out into the passing lane with lights flashing all over the place. He passed the car between us, and he accelerated like a bad dog. Then, and only then, did I put on my brakes. I was already in a deceleration mode, and he was in an acceleration mode. The two speeds were not equal, because in one second, he was going faster, and I was going slower. The Corvette had incredible brakes, four wheel disk, and radial ply tires. My car was coming to an abrupt stop, and the CHP, not so much so.

Finally, he realized that I was pulling over, so he set his brakes. The ass end of his car lifted up high into the air, and I watched him fishtail, trying to keep control of his Detroit Iron. This was before anti-lock brakes. His front tires locked and clouds of billowing plumes of burned rubber permeating the area. He was all over the place. He put the car in reverse and stopped about fifty feet in front of us. I had already pulled over, turned the motor off and set the parking brake. So I released the brake, started the motor and drove toward him. The parking break handle was under the dash, so at that point we had a misunderstanding. I meant to turn on the parking lights, but the headlights came on. At that moment, I noticed both police officers were going for their guns. *No more misunderstandings!* I turned off the lights and motor and left it in gear. I wasn't going to set the parking brake again. I put my hands on top of the windshield frame and told my fellow Marine to do the same. He asked, "What?" I said, "Put your hands up." He followed my lead.

The driver of the police car — we can now call him "Sir" — seemed a bit agitated. He was acting like a Marine Corps Drill Instructor. It was as though his one and only dog had just died, and his wife had given him the clap, while having an affair with his best friend. Suffice it to say, he was not happy. Of course, now he politely asked us to get out of the car, but it sounded something like this: "Get out of the car NOW!" There was a great deal of emphasis on the "NOW!" With our hands in the air, it seemed a very good idea to do as he suggested. They spread eagled us out on the car and got intimate. I don't smoke, but I felt I should have a cigarette after he was done. They were searching us for weapons. We had none. Sir asked us nicely if we had any weapons, drugs or booze in the car and if they could search. I assured Sir that we did not, but the only answer at this time was, "Yes, of course, Sir. Go ahead." We were clean. Sir searched the car while the other police officer had us under guard off to the shoulder of the road. Then, he asked what I was doing with my hand under the dash. Yeah — he saw that. I pointed to the hand brake and told him I was releasing the brake. He actually seemed to understand. Sir asked for my driver's license and registration. I showed him my license, registration and my military I.D. Then, he asked about the military I.D, "What's this?" I told him that I was under orders from the Marine Corps to always show my I.D. if I had any encounters with law enforcement. Sir disappeared into his Detroit Iron and did a quick radio check on me, my partner in crime and my car. He was searching for any wants or warrants. All the searches came back clean, and the demeanor of Sir changed. He wasn't yelling anymore and didn't seem totally pissed off – a good sign. He asked me where I going in such a hurry. I lied and told him we were trying to get back to base before our liberty was up. He wanted to know where we were stationed. I told him Twenty-nine Palms. He was familiar with the place.

Now begins a tap dance that would have put *Dancing with the Stars* to shame. While I was figuratively polishing his badge, shining his shoes and kissing his ass, he asked why I was in the passing lane and how fast I was going. I explained that I was passing car number one and was going to pull back in. Then, I saw his car coming out onto the road and thought it would take him awhile to accelerate. I didn't want to go back in my lane and then slam on my brakes to avoid his car. So I decided to stay in the passing lane to pass him and the next car in line. After all, it was a wide open stretch of road, with good visibility and dry surfaces. He asked, "Didn't you see I was the CHP?" I answered, "Not until I passed you, sir." He continued, "How fast were you going?" I replied, "Sir, I had my full concentration on the road and driving. I wasn't looking at the speedometer." He said, and I shit you not, "You must have been going at least 120 mph." Damn good eyes on that cop. I said, "No, no. I'm sure I wasn't going *that* fast." He said, "Well, you have to admit you were going at least 100 mph. *Right?" Phwee!* Now we were negotiating. I said, "No, I don't think I was going *that* fast." We talked and talked, and finally, we both began to smile a bit. I wasn't going to admit to a damn thing and he knew it. He didn't have a speed gun and didn't track me long enough to get an accurate speed. By now, we were both chatting and smiling a lot more. I told him I had been to Vietnam and a little about the Corps – how anything he could do would pale in comparison to the Corps' punishment. Finally, Sir grew sterner and said, "I am going to give you a ticket for doing 70 in a 65. You can go to court and beat it if you want, but I wouldn't if I were you, "WE KNOW THIS CAR." The same words the MP said to me the first night I arrived on base. I promised him I would not contest it. When the ticket came in the mail, a few fellow Marines said, "Fight it in court. You'll win," but I paid the ticket and honored my word to the CHP. My Guardian Angel again.

The Desert

In Vietnam, it was hot and humid, with vegetation everywhere and a bunch of little Gomers running about trying to end what would otherwise be a perfectly good day. Twenty-nine Palms was hot too, but it was dry with little vegetation and no jungle anywhere. With the exception of the ambush trap I spoke of earlier, no one seemed to want to terminate me. In addition, I had always had trouble with my sinuses. I would catch a cold, and it would become sinusitis and stay with me for months. I didn't know what it was then. I just knew that when I caught colds, they lasted a long time and hurt. I caught one cold while at Twenty-nine Palms. It started on a Tuesday and was gone by Thursday.

The Corps provided me with good chow, a place to stay and the opportunity to save some money. The only thing lacking was female companionship, so I went out on a reconnaissance mission and found some.

While I was there, I made Sergeant, and I did it in twenty-nine months. It was a very fast progression. Why not one-hundred percent, right? My CO (Commanding Officer) called me into his office along with the senior ranking NCO (Non-Commissioned Officer). They had a career briefing with me and offered me OCS (Officer's Candidate School) and Aviation. A chance to become a pilot? Really? After my first experience flying to boot camp, that would have been a dream come true. A dream, as I said earlier, I had secretly held all my life. So, I looked into the program. The first thing the Corps wanted me to do was "ship for six" – reenlist for six years. There was a bit of confusion on my part. I thought I was going to be an officer. They explained that if I wasn't selected to go to OCS, I would return to my enlisted rank for six more years. Once I became an officer, the commitment would be replaced with a four-year officer's commitment, but first I had to apply to OCS and be accepted. If I wasn't accepted, I had just reenlisted for six more years. I asked, "If I am selected, then what happens?" First, they replied, I would have to successfully complete OCS and agree to accept "if offered" a commission. *Say what?* Just a damned second here. You mean, I can be selected, successfully complete the program, and *not* be offered a commission? Yes, that's right. And I had just enlisted for six more years. So, then what? After I became a "conditional" or, I think it was, a "probationary" officer, I would attend a six-month school called TBS (The Basic School). All Marine

Corps Officers go through TBS. It is a shared experience. Actually, it is a very good concept as you'll learn later, and of course, if I didn't pass TBS, I had just reenlisted for six more years.

The little hairs on the back of my neck were jumping all over the place and then stood at full attention. *Whoa! DANGER, Will Robinson!* I actually thought about it for a very short while – less than a month. I was conflicted, "Why not 100%?" came up against the possibility of a booby trap. I remembered my first experience with a Marine Corps Recruiter. Once bitten, twice shy.

The question became moot. I received orders to Camp Smith, Hawaii – a reward for making Sergeant in short order. One man's treasure is another man's trash.

I wasn't really all that happy about leaving The Stumps – a loving nickname given to Twenty-nine Palms. I left the desert behind and the company of a close female Marine. I drove the Corvette home, avoiding Amboy on the way. I got home, sold the car and got myself a brand new VW Beetle. It had better gas mileage, less maintenance, and there was nowhere to drive 120 mph on the island. Besides, I was passed by more damn VW's than you can imagine. The reason was that the CHP didn't see them, but they knew my car. I really liked my little VW and dreamed of owning a Porsche 912 or 911 someday. Dreams can come true after all, can't they?

I incurred a short additional active duty service commitment for moving to Hawaii. It was called a PCS (Permanent Change of Station).

PTSD

I arrived in Hawaii in May of 1970. Didn't like it at all. Camp Smith was Headquarters for all of the Pacific – all land, air and sea assets. They were more than a little uptight. I wasn't. My car arrived, and I drove all the way around the island the second week I was there. I was trapped on a very small island surrounded by water, and I was aware of it. I didn't know what was going on with me.

Camp Smith was up in mountains, sitting in the middle of the rain forest and jungle. It was hot enough and humid, and the hairs on the back of my neck began to rise daily. There were a bunch of Asians in Hawaii. I felt I was in danger. I couldn't even go into the market place downtown. The noises, the chatter and the goods for sale were all Asian, and I was in fear for my life. All signs, I would find out later, pointed to PTSD (Post-Traumatic-Stress-Disorder).

While I had never been anything other than a top notch Marine, in Hawaii I was getting chewed out by my NCOIC and then my OIC — and not just once. I was told my hair was too long. I went to the barber shop and told them to give me a regulation Marine Corps haircut. They did, and my Major told me to go back to the barber shop and get another one. Nothing I did seemed to be right. Everything, it seemed, was wrong.

While I had been one of the most liked Marines at Twenty-nine Palms, here they shunned me. They thought I had "shipped for six" to make sergeant and get to Hawaii. They thought I was a "Lifer." A Lifer is someone who can't make it on the outside. It is said by Marines that they are like flies, "They eat shit and bother people." The question of OCS was totally off the board.

With the exception of going to a military beach to body surf, I stayed on base. Then, the Marine Corps started offering an "Early Out" program. I went to personnel and asked about it. They checked my records and said I should have been told about it before my PCS. I really don't recall them saying anything about it, but they looked at my records and said I could get out early if I wanted to. I wanted to and as we will see later it turned into another incredible stroke of good luck. My Guardian Angel, always watching over me.

Leaving the Corps

From Hawaii, I went to Treasure Island, California, in the San Francisco Bay. It was an out-processing facility. The Marines that were there seemed to have a bad taste in their mouths. Those of us separating from the Corps were beginning to rebel — not blousing our pants and, generally, getting a little out of line. A grumpy old Gunny called me into his office one day. His Lance Corporal, enlisted pay grade E3 (a troop handler) had identified me as the ring leader. They got that right — always the leader. I had cleaned crappers the first week in the Marines, and here I am in my last week, a Sergeant E5, being told to clean the heads by some dipshit E3 with an earring hole in his head. *Not going to happen.* The Gunny said if I didn't cooperate that he could put my folder at the bottom of the pile. He also seemed to be pissed that I was leaving the Marines, saying, "You got a problem with *my* Marine Corps?" The Corps doesn't like a quitter. Finally, we received our paperwork. They gave us a ride to the main gate with a military escort, concerned we might want to return and try to enact revenge. I didn't even look back.

Summer

In Summer, all the creeks and streams join together to make a swiftly flow-ing river. The waters are turbulent, wild and refuse to remain inside their banks. They will not be contained. They are free and flowing and now with great strength and force.

School

I am now out of the Corps. It is summer and I'm living my fifth year of high school. I thought everyone had changed but me, but I quickly realized that it was me, and not them, who had changed. I noticed this particularly with a few friends who had not gone off to the military or if they had, did not go to Vietnam.

I took the summer off. I tried for a while to fit in, but there was a pecking order in high school, and I wasn't about to be put into anyone's order – not anymore. I had learned a lot of good life lessons by now. I had been a Sergeant in the United States Marine Corps and a veteran of the Vietnam War, and that was enough. It meant something to me.

I decided to become a student. In high school, I wasn't much of one, as you may remember, but the VA (Veterans Administration) was going to pay me to go to school. I didn't have a job, and my parents – actually, my father – said I could stay with them without paying room or board, as long as I was going to school and getting the grades. By the way he quit drinking. Doctor told him it was killing him.

It was too late for me to sign up for the fall term, so I took an evening ac-counting class at a local business school. Time and money wasted. I did meet a young woman there. She worked during the day and went to school at night. She had an apartment, and I did not, so we spent some time there. We dated and then broke up after a short period of time.

I went to register for winter term at PCC (Portland Community College) – an excellent school at the time. I put together a complete class schedule and went around to each table to sign up. The classes were all closed. They had enough students. Students from the fall term got first chance at all the vacant class seats for the winter term. So, now I was scrambling to find some classes to take. The only classes available were night classes. Again, the hand of my Angel stepped in.

Because I was living at home, my parents and I were bound to cross paths. By going to night school, I would leave in the late afternoon before they got home. I would then go to class until 10 pm or later, and when I returned, they were asleep in bed. I would study until about 2 am each morning, and then I would go to bed. My parents would get up in the morning and leave for work before I got up. Then, I would get up, eat, do more homework and leave again. I lived like this for about two years. We seldom saw each other. It was a good arrangement.

The people in the night classes were older and more serious about learning. The classes were smaller, the campus more quiet, and the instructors took an interest in their students. They wanted me to succeed, and so did I. My mantra was, "Why not a hundred percent," as I embarked on a one-hundred eighty hour march. During the first and second terms, I had to take a bonehead class in math to get me up to speed. In the first term, I only took twelve hours of classes, only nine of which would transfer to a four year college. I got great grades, but as I looked at those nine hours, I realized that this was going to be a hump. I had no idea. *One foot in front of the other, Marine.*

I ran into Barry at night school. We knew each other from high school, and we had actually bumped into each other once while in Vietnam, on Hill 55. Yes, he too was a former Marine. We were serious about school. I noticed that I was seeing less and less of my friends from the old days, and then I turned my back on all of them. It just needed to be done, and it wasn't the hardest thing I've ever done. They were holding me back, and I knew it.

Dan was my best friend throughout grade and high school. He and I had gone off to the Marines together. He got his right leg blown off above the knee when he had less than a month to go in Vietnam. He told me later, after he tried to commit suicide that he wished he had died that day in Vietnam. It messed him up for life. We had a grade school class reunion in 2002, and it was the first time I had spoken with Dan in over thirty years. He said, "I was pissed off at you for getting your shit together while the rest of us weren't." I was reminded of a bucket full of crabs, all trying to escape their captivity. One would get right up to the edge – so close to freedom – and then the other crabs would pull him back in. I escaped the crab bucket.

It was during my second year at PCC when I noticed a table with AFROTC (Air Force Reserve Officer Training Corps) cadets sitting around. At first, I laughed and passed them by. Then, I wondered what they might have to say. What about flying? I talked to a cadet and picked up some literature about the program. It was then that I noticed the same wording, "Agree to accept if offered." I found out the Air Force was offering a commission to just about everyone who graduated. The cadets gave me a schedule of events. First, there was testing, six-parts, including Math, Science, English and Leadership in the morning and Pilot and Navigator suitability in the afternoon. You had to score at least in the top twenty-fifth percentile on all the morning tests. The pilot and navigator tests were optional. Yes – I took both. I did extremely well (the high ninety-sixth percentile) in the Leadership testing – having been a Marine Corps Sergeant, Vietnam War Veteran and all. *Ya think?* I did well on both Science and English, scoring somewhere in the mid-fifties. But on the Math portion, I only scored in the eighteenth percentile. Not good enough – or was it? The Air Force needed bodies in 1972, and they were offering a waiver. You could score in the fifteenth percentile or higher in one: English, Math or Science, but not in leadership. I scored in the ninety-eighth percentile on the Pilot testing and in the ninety-second percentile for Navigator testing. *Oh-my-gosh, I had passed!* Thank you, Guardian Angel!

From the time that I turned six, my mother kept asking me, "What's your plan? What are you going to do with your life? You have to have a plan." In my second year at PCC I told my mother my plan. I was going to get my degree, go to pilot training, finish a career in the Air Force and then fly for an airline. She said, "Well plans don't always work out the way you want them to." *Really,* Mother? *Wow – just wow.*

I read up on all the requirements for the physical. One of the requirements was a "maximum" sitting height. *What's that?* I wondered. So, I sat up all proud and had my mother measure me. I was one half-inch too tall to go to pilot training. *What?!* The whole deal was off if I couldn't go to UPT (Undergraduate Pilot Training). Seems that if you have to punch out of your aircraft, your head would go through the canopy, before the canopy piercing tool. So, if I had to punch out at UPT, I would have in all likelihood broken my neck. Instead, I crouched when I sat and came out one quarter-inch below the limit. I practiced over and over again until I could do it just by the way it felt.

I went for my physical exam and the airman administering the test told me to, "Sit up straight." I told him, "I am sitting up straight." He told me three times and measured me three times. When he was finished, I asked him how I had done. He said, "If you were one-quarter of an inch taller you wouldn't be going to UPT." I asked, "You mean to tell me there *is* a maximum sitting height?" He replied, "Yes." How badly did I want to fly? Well, I was willing to risk my life for it – that's how bad.

I was majoring in Business Administration and getting great grades. I had one of the worst guidance counselors in history. He tried to tell me what I wanted and didn't want. All I wanted him to tell me was how to do what I wanted to do. I told him I wanted to go into the Air Force to fly. "Oh, no!" he exclaimed, "You don't want to do *that!*" I said, "Yes, I do." Eventually, I convinced him that I did. But this was during the Vietnam War, when campuses were very anti-military. So, when I asked him about transferring hours to a four-year college, he gave me less than accurate information.

I was now taking a lot more than fifteen hours a term – just trying to catch up. I applied to the UO (University of Oregon). It was the only school I applied to. I looked at school requirements for both the UO and Oregon State. I found Oregon State was a lot more structured, and that structure would make it more difficult for me to graduate in time so I didn't apply. Barry was going to the UO and was accepted in July 1972. I didn't get accepted until late August, but accepted I was. Barry and I roomed together for two years.

I joined AFROTC and talked on the phone with the PAS (Professor of Aerospace Studies). He was a Full Bird Colonel, officer grade O-6. He was excited to have me coming. There is only one time you can make a first impression, so I showed up with my hair down to my shoulders and mutton chops. He asked from another room, "Is that my Marine out there?" He welcomed me and then gave me a look. We talked for a while, and then he said, "You do realize we have appearance requirement standards right?" I kind of chuckled to myself and said, "Yes, Sir, I do, and I will be squared away come Day One." I went to the barbershop and got most everything cut off. Come Day One, I looked like a squared-away Marine. I figured I would start at the bottom and work my way up, I don't recommend that.

I did a few things right away in ROTC that caught the attention of all the staff, showing that I could and did get things done. I was quickly working my way through the ranks of AFROTC.

My academic questions and transfer from PCC now came back to haunt me. Yes, I had good enough grades for the Business School at the university, but there were prerequisite classes needed that were only offered at the UO. My counselor didn't tell me that. The university said, "Not a problem. Just take the classes this year, and *then* apply to the Business School." *No problem?* He had just told me it would take me an extra year to graduate.

Well, that was problem – a *huge* problem. I had to commission before my twenty-sixth birthday and enter pilot training before age twenty-six-and-a-half. As it was, I was up against the wall, time-wise. All my plans went down the drain. I couldn't finish my business degree *and* graduate in time for the Air Force. What could I do? I looked around at other majors and nothing seemed to work. Then, I found a major called "General Social Sciences." I checked the requirements. The only major requirement was to be accepted by the University – not a school within the University. I would have to have at least seventy-two hours in Social Sciences – four disciplines had to have at least twelve hours in each. I reviewed my Social Sciences credits from PCC, and there were scant few. But I did the math, and it would work – if I did.

My junior year, the Air Force wanted another physical – eyes only, this time. We drove from Eugene, Oregon to McChord AFB, Washington. It was about a five-hour drive. The next morning, I took a test to check my refectory error. That is the test where they ask, "Which one is clearer, number one or number two?" I failed the test and lost my 1P (UPT) status. The staff at the detachment told me I was still qualified to be a navigator, but I didn't want to be a passenger. I wanted to fly! I went to one of the administration clerks and asked, "Is there anything I can do?" He said, "There is absolutely nothing you can do." I asked, "Nothing?" He repeated himself. I said, "There *has* to be something." He said, "Well, you *could* request a waiver, but I'm not going to go through the paperwork for you, because they will just reject it. I have never seen a waiver approved for this problem." So, there *was* something I could do. I could request a waiver. I told him I would do all of the paperwork myself. I found the regulation to request a waiver, wrote a letter and got the PAS to sign it on my behalf, and sweet-talked the civilian typist in the office to type up the entire package. She said, she wasn't supposed to help me, but she did. Sometimes it pays to *not* be an asshole.

I submitted the paperwork and waited. After a month went by, I asked the NCO if there was any word. He said, "No," and followed it up with a disgusted look which said, "Why are you wasting my time?" It was just my life – that was all. I asked a couple more times and got the same response. Then, about six weeks after the request was submitted, I walked into the office. The NCO said, "I can't ****in' believe it. They approved your request. That has *never* happened before. This is not a waiver-able item." He was dumbfounded. I just had a feeling it would work out. My Guardian Angel.

The Air Force was always giving physical tests of some sort. My senior year, close to graduation, I was told I would have to go to Kingsley Field in Klamath Falls, Oregon for another eye test. I would have to drive through the mountains in the winter – sounded like a good plan to me. I took all the normal eye tests. One I always had trouble with was the "Depth Perception Test." The test consisted of two columns, with three sets of five round circles in a line. I was supposed to identify which one of the five circles was closest to me, but I was doing terrible on the test. The airman giving the test said, "I'll give you a hint, none of them are one or five." Okay, I had just narrowed the field down to three. The problem was that each set of five circles got progressively more difficult as you went along. I finished the test. The airman said, "You failed the test, but I'm going to pass you anyway. I'm getting out of the Air Force, and I just don't care anymore." *I-shit-you-not!* My Guardian Angel, with me always.

There were two women in our class. One of them, Laura Lynn took a liking to me. She knew I had a girlfriend in Portland, so her logic was to set me up with one of her sorority sisters so that maybe I would forget about Portland and eventually date her. It was a faulty logic and didn't work out the way she had expected. I did say I would go, but asked, "Does your sister bark and wag her tail?" Not so funny. So, I met my date, and she wasn't a dog at all. I noticed, however, that she was somewhat *cool* toward me. As the night progressed, I asked my date what Laura Lynn had told her about me. She said, "You mean besides asking if I barked and wagged my tail?" I had a lot of ground to make up. The Fall Festival Dance we attended was in October of 1972. I married my blind date in July of 1974, and we recently celebrated our forty-first wedding anniversary. Laura Lynn was a big part of our lives. Sadly, she died a few years ago.

My junior year went very well in ROTC and I was selected to be the Cadet Corps Commander, fall term of my senior year – the top cadet position within the corps. My job was to interface with the staff and students and to run the program. That took a lot of time, but I was keeping up grades – something the counselor at PCC said I wouldn't be able to do.

At the beginning of my senior year, one of the admin NCO's, the same one who told me my waiver wouldn't be approved, came to me and said, "You're not going to make it, you need seventy-three hours to graduate on time." A normal class year was forty-five hours. Essentially, I needed to complete five terms in three. I assured him I would. He said, "There's no way." *Yeah, just like the waiver, right?* I took twenty-four hours fall term and was the Cadet Corps Commander. I earned a 3.45 GPA that term. Winter term came, and I took twenty-eight hours and completed my private pilot's license at the same time (a requirement to go to UPT). That was also time-consuming. I ended with a 3.4 GPA that term. During my final term, I took twenty-four hours, needing only twenty-one to graduate. I dropped one of the classes at the end of the term. I needed one-hundred eighty hours total, seventy-two in major and forty eight in four disciplines and that was exactly what I had – the bare minimum. ROTC helped me out. They gave me six hours of credit for my time in the Marines. I graduated number one in the AFROTC class and won the academic excellence award with a cumulative 3.43 GPA. I was also a "Distinguished Graduate" – the only one the University of Oregon AFROTC program had that year. It would prove to be an important accomplishment.

I Am Going to UPT! Or Am I?

The year I graduated, the Air Force decreased the number of pilot training slots by about twenty percent. As a Distinguished Graduate, I was supposed to be first to go and get my choice of bases. Of course, I wanted to go to "Willie" (Williams AFB in Phoenix, Arizona). The Captain called me in one day and asked me, "Where do you really want to go to pilot training?" I thought for a split second. *What was this? A booby trap?* So, I replied, "It doesn't really matter where I go just as long as I get to go." He said, "Todd, you're going to go a long ways in the Air Force." There was also supposed to be a delay, but I asked for a hardship waiver for an expedited active duty induction date. I asked the Colonel to sign off on it, he did, and it was approved.

I got my orders. We were going to Webb AFB, Big Spring, Texas. I was going to be a Social Actions Officer until Pilot Training. I was nervous. Had they finally set the trap and caught me?

My wife and I arrived in Big Spring at night, and it was all lit up. We thought maybe this wouldn't be as bad as we had heard. We woke up the next morning and found the lights were from an oil refinery. The town and area around it smelled like rotten eggs – the oil from the oil fields causes this to happen. It *was* as bad as we had heard.

I was a Social Actions Officer for three-and-a-half months. I sat in my office watching T-37's and T-38's taking off and landing. I did well in Social Actions. Social Actions was a new program, and I wrote the job description for an action officer for all of ATC (Air Training Command). It was my job to insure that an individual's ability to proceed and advance was not impeded due to race, creed, color, national origin or sex. I handled about twenty cases of alleged discrimination. Two were found valid.

One Thursday afternoon, as I was doing my staff work, administration came down with a new set of orders. "Assigned to UPT Class 76-07 starting in March 1975." I had three days to get ready, but I was more than ready. Were they *really* going to let me fly their multi-million dollar airplanes? *Really? YES!*

We knew there would still be a number of hoops to jump through. The first was to give us another physical exam with more eye tests, including the depth perception test. They had us wait in line. My turn was next, and they asked the guy in front of me to read off the closest circles. He read them so quickly, I almost didn't have time to write them on the napkin I had in my hand, but I did. I held the napkin in my left hand and cheated. I passed the test. How bad did I really want to fly? You have no idea!

Oh, in thirty-two years of flying I never once had trouble finding the ground. It was always below me.

There were twenty in our class. We spent two weeks in academics and physical training before going to the flight line. I didn't have any trouble with that. The PT test was easy enough with the exception of the pull-ups. I knew what the requirements were. We had to do at least eleven pull-ups. I worked out every single day until I could do at least fifteen, on some days, seventeen. One of our students hung on the bar unable to do one single pull up. He knew what the requirements were and was washed out of the program before we hit the flight line. He didn't want it, I did.

After two weeks, we were reassigned to the flight line. Nothing could prepare you for it. It was like trying to take a sip of water from a fire hose turned on full blast. It came quickly – the academics, the flying and, of course, the initiation. The instructors weren't going to just teach us how to fly, but give us all crap to join their fraternity. The fact that I was a prior Marine didn't help my case at all. In fact, I think it hurt it.

Day One, they told us if you have trouble with the flying we will get you through the program, but if you don't study and know your stuff, you're gone. Well, "Why not a hundred percent", "Task Completion" and "I will never quit", all kicked back in.

I met Mac on Day One. He would become my best friend for the next thirty-two years. It seemed an unlikely friendship, I am told – he was Irish Catholic, and I was English Protestant. We didn't know we weren't supposed to be friends, so we were, and what a friendship it was! Every man needs a male friend he can go to for encouragement and to tell him when he is screwing up – to give and to take advice. Mac was that person. We shared so many interests. He and I were both into Porsches, music and becoming pilots. We used to sit across the table and "pimp" (ask questions) each other for hours. It was called "chair flying," do in a chair what you would do in the plane. Each morning before we would fly, the staff would have a formal briefing. They would ask all kinds of questions: Bold Face (memory items), procedures, limitation, systems knowledge, and everything else.

Each class had its own designation. Ours was 76-07, which meant we would be the seventh graduating class of 1976. On a wall in the administration building, there was a display with a set of wings and the names of those who started the class under the wings. When a pilot would washout (fail), they would remove the wings and leave the name there. Incentive? I think they would call it that. We lost four of our twenty: One for the PT, one for academics, one for his inability to learn (he couldn't fly), and one for manifestation of apprehension (fear of flying). The latter kept getting air sick every time he went up. My buddy Mac got sick well into T-38's, didn't pass the final physical training test for running and failed one too many academic tests. He graduated along with me. His Guardian Angel with him as was mine. Always.

They gave us a "dollar ride" – the first flight in the aircraft. There is no real instruction, we just went up and experienced how it felt. They took us up and tried to get us airsick. My instructor turned the airplane upside down and inside out. A piece of FOD (Foreign Object Damage), a washer, kept getting loose in the cockpit, so the instructor turned the airplane upside-down and pumped the stick repeatedly to dislodge it. Actually, he was trying his best to get me airsick. I didn't get sick that day nor any day in the thirty-two years that I flew. They called me a "virgin."

A student *could* quit the program – it was called SIE (Self-Initiated Elimination). I would never do that. I would rather die first. I studied hard and succeeded. The T-37 was a side-by-side aircraft where the instructor sat next to the trainee, so it felt like a team. I finished close to the top of the class. The T-38 was a different matter. It is tandem – the instructor sits behind the trainee. It always felt like he was looking over my shoulder. Well, because that was exactly what he was doing. I finished last in the class in T-38's. I busted a couple of in-flight evaluations. I was almost washed out. They called me in for a ground evaluation which lasted about two hours. They asked me everything there was to know about the airplane, flying, regulations, etc. They covered it all. In two hours, I think I only got two of the questions wrong. I knew my stuff.

The T-37

The T-38

I could spend hours telling you about the flying, the comradery, the shots of adrenalin I got every time I took-off or landed, and the in-flight emergencies. I was a hooked junkie. My drug was flying.

Chuck Yeager broke the sound barrier in 1947 – the first pilot to ever do so. Thousands would follow in his path. I broke it in 1976, in a T-38, my hands flying the controls. No one can take that away from me.

ATC had a new program. They wanted every student to get the plane they requested in place of the one that was assigned to them. I had been to Vietnam and had flown with an Air Force C-130 crew, and they were having fun. I liked fun. My philosophy of flying was simple, "Do it safe, get it done, and have fun."

C-130 Air Force pilots in Vietnam flew in shorts, tennis shoes, green t-shirts and baseball caps. That was the war-time Air Force: do your job, and don't sweat the small stuff. Everything other than flying was the small stuff.

The Christmas prior to graduation, my wife and I drove to several Air Force bases in Texas: a MAC (Military Airlift Command) base where they hauled cargo and personnel, a SAC (Strategic Air Command) base where their mission was long range bombers and air refueling, and a TAC (Tactical Air Command) base where their mission was fighters. I observed that the MAC base seemed some-what relaxed. The SAC base was really uptight. The TAC base, well, they were a bunch of total and complete assholes. In their defense, we got there on New Year's Eve. At times, I can be an asshole too. Some have said I am very good at it, but I didn't raise to the TAC level. So, based on that information, I decided I would request a C-130. I also put on my "dream sheet" (requested duty assignment) that I was a volunteer for overseas.

I went to see Captain Garrison the class commander. We were going to decide which airplane I would request so that everyone could get their first choice, and make the numbers look good. He asked me what I wanted to fly, and I replied, "A C-130." He said, "That's good. You're a good stick, but you have had some problems with check rides," and then said, and I quote, "We wouldn't want you to hurt yourself or damage any Air Force Equipment." What a prick! After all the work I had done, he could have just said, "I think that's good choice." I didn't mention before, but he was a fighter pilot on loan from TAC to ATC.

That day, I flew two missions, a.k.a. "sorties." Both were good rides. When I got back to the squad bay, I was told the Captain wanted to see me again. I went in and closed the door. He said, "I have some great news for you. There is an F-4 remaining in our block, and it's yours if you want it." I thought, *Damn! Those two rides today must have been fantastic.* I asked, "Does this mean I don't get my C-130?" He looked a little shocked and said, "You can have it if you want it." To which I replied, "I do. After all, I wouldn't want to hurt myself or damage any Air Force Equipment." Then, I left the room. By the way, they coerced another pilot, who wanted a C-141 to McChord to take the F-4. I think he has forgiven me by now. I talk with him on occasion.

I got my wings. I'm going to fly.

The C-130

The C-130 school was in Jacksonville, Arkansas, close to Little Rock. I left my wife in Big Spring with all our stuff. She had a job and wouldn't have had anything to do in Arkansas anyway. The class was three-and-a-half months long.

A lot of the pilots in my class didn't want to be there. They thought they should be flying fighters. I was fine with it all. I didn't like the room where we stayed. I found the TV and refrigerator distracted me, so I pulled the plugs on both.

The training was divided into what would become a normal syllabus. First, you had ground school with a lot of tests. Then, there was an oral exam, followed by the flight simulator. Our simulator was a relic. Later, they would replace it with a state of the art, six-axis full-motion simulator – and an incredibly video game. Ours had none of that. We called it the "Box" and still do. Inside the Box, anything that can go wrong does go wrong. There were always lights, bells and whistles going off. Our job was to identify what was going wrong and why. This while still flying the plane. But unlike a single-seat fighter, there are two pilots to share the workload and a flight engineer. At first, I hated the Box. It didn't fly like an airplane. Later, I learned to love it. It was a challenge, and I got good at it, really good!

Next was the flying. It was divided into two parts. First, the basic school, where they taught you how to fly and land the plane. Actually, it took two hands to fly. It was a handful – kind of like driving a very big truck. My buddy Mac called it a "Dempsey Dumpster" in the sky. I called it the "Herk," the C-130 being the "Hercules."

By the way, Mac got a T-37 to Sacramento, California. The T-37 is a Boeing 737. He had no intention of staying in the Air Force. For him, it was only a means to an end to fly commercially.

I was having trouble landing the Herk. The instructor did what he could do. I went home one night and landed over a hundred times in my room. The next day I came out and there were no problems flying or landing. The instructor was dumbfounded and asked how and where I learned to land the airplane. I told him what I had done. All he could say was, "Really? I'll put that into my bag of tricks."

The "bag of tricks" was what an instructor pilot would use to teach a student. If one thing didn't work, you would reach into your bag and try something else. You never quit, and you never gave up on a student.

I did really well on the check ride in the Herk. The check airman said it was near flawless with only a couple of points to discuss. Check airmen feel they have to do that in order to do their job.

Next was the tactical portion of the training. First, a little ground school. Then, how to fly in formation and drop perfectly good people and equipment out of the back. When they found out I was going to Alaska, they paired me with Major Phil who was also going to Elmendorf AFB in Anchorage. He thought he was going there to be the Squadron Operations Officer, number two in the squadron. That didn't work out. We settled down to learn how to fly tactical, which is the main bread and butter of the Herk.

The major had flown the KC-135, a refueler, and the Herk during Vietnam. The Herk squadron was actually located at a base in a distant place called CCK (Ching Chuan Kang Air Base) located in Taichung, Taiwan. I would hear stories about CCK mentioned so many times in the coming years. We did okay in tactical. We didn't set the world on fire, but we both passed our check rides.

Then, it was back to Big Spring to pick up my wife and head out. Not so fast. There was a shortage of on and off-base housing in Alaska. The Alaska pipeline was in full swing. So my orders were to go to Elmendorf for a two-year, unaccompanied (without my wife) assignment. I drove cross country in a 1970 911T Porsche. I had purchased it about two weeks before I got my assignment. The 911T was only six years old at the time, but she was worn out – abused, actually. No need for the abuse. An air-cooled engine in Alaska was not a great idea. I kept it for a while, and then said I was done with Porsches. As we will see later, that wasn't the case.

I stayed at my parent's place for a couple of days in Portland. Then, I called Mac to see if he wanted some company. His answer was the same as always, "Of course! When are you going to be here?" I drove to Sacramento and visited for three days. Then I drove to Seattle to put my car on the boat. I flew to Alaska and a new adventure in my life.

When I got there, it was late August and had already started to get cold early in the night. It was about two weeks before we got "termination dust." Termination dust was our term for the first snow of the season.

I checked in with billeting, got a room and checked on the status of housing. There was still none. I was told that if I could get someone to say my wife could stay with them, she could come. In conversation, I told Major Phil about the housing issue. He said he and "Fatty," his wife (who was anything but fat) would sign saying my wife had a place to stay. My wife was then on her way to Alaska and me.

I told her to get some winter clothes. She got dressed up for winter in Texas, not Alaska. She had these cute boots with about an eighth of an inch insulation. She saw what other women were wearing and said, "I won't have anything to do with it." Two weeks later, we got her a new wardrobe, including Sorel boots and a huge parka. She would wear them for the next five years.

Then, my commitment in Alaska changed to three years. I stayed for five years. I started flying the Herk in Alaska. Oh my God! I was always visual, but this was incredible. The landscapes beyond the horizon cannot be described.

SOS

Just prior to my upgrade to Captain, I was selected to go to SOS (Squadron Officer's School). It is one of three service schools the Air Force has, the others being Air Command and Staff, and Air War college.

I flew to Portland, bought a new Honda Accord and drove to Montgomery, Alabama. The first day of class, we were supposed to tell a few things about ourselves. Our class instructor got up and said, "I wear the Red Pants. (The instructors wore Red Pants on the athletic fields). That makes me one of the bad guys." *Strike One*. Then, "I'm just another dumb throttle jockey," – meaning anyone who flies is dumb. *Strike Two*. And finally, "When I graduated from pilot training, our class got a really bad block of airplanes, and I got stuck with a C-130." *Strike Three*." When it came my turn to say something about myself, I said, "What can I say, I'm just another dumb C-130 throttle jockey." My SOS experience went downhill from there. I was known to be able to cop an attitude. I felt attacked, because I was being attacked, and I copped an attitude.

I did very well in academics and the field work. In leadership, Mr. Red Pants gave me an evaluation that put me towards the bottom twenty-fifth percentile of the class. His evaluation had more weight than the others, but I graduated and not in the bottom fifteenth percent. I found out later that being in the bottom fifteenth percentile put you on some sort of shit list.

Flying the Herk

The C-130 Hercules

In 1978, I went straight from SOS to Captain up-grade in Little Rock. The training was easy this time. I was getting a lot better at this flying thing.

I really learned how to fly in Alaska. Your pilot wings just make pilots dangerous and liable enough to get into trouble. I did very well flying the C-130 in Alaska. I upgraded to Captain in two short years. Then, I started to have some problems with check rides. The higher-ups finally figured it out. I had developed

"Check-I-Tis," the fear of check rides. So, they started showing up with "no no-tice" check rides. You didn't know ahead of time they were coming, so there was nothing to lose sleep over the night before. I believe I had eight to ten of them in about eight months. All were glowing, and I got over my fear. From then on, there were no more problems. It was 1978, and I had another check ride that day. I did extremely well and I was a little full of myself.

Then, events occurred which would change things forever for me. I got a call from SSgt Steve saying there had been a crash at Sparrevohn Air Force Station. Not to worry, it was a C-130 from the rescue squadron, not from our airlift squadron, the 17th. A short time later, he called back and said it was one of our planes. He gave me the names of the crew. The captain was a colorful pilot nicknamed *Mad Dog*. He was called that because most everyone thought he was a little off-center. He had a great sense of humor. He would show up on occasion at a formal commander's call with a dead chicken carcass on his head. He was a character. He had also been my instructor at the tactical school in Little Rock in 1976. He was one of the best sticks and pilots I ever flew with. I liked and admired the man. He was now dead. If it could happen to Mad Dog, it could happen to anyone. It could happen to me, which caused me a little sobering up.

We had four airstrips in Alaska that we called "one way" strips. There was only one way in and the opposite way out. You would land, unload, reload, do a one-hundred-and-eighty-degree turn on the ground, and fly off in the opposite direction. These same four airstrips were into boxed canyons. After a certain point, you could no longer execute a missed approach and go around. You were committed to land. We called them, "Two Capes and a Spare Indian." They were Cape Romanzof, Cape Newenham, Sparrevohn and Indian Mountain.

Mad Dog had gotten too deep into the canyon, lost sight of the runway, and elected to go around. Bad choice. He may have made it if the co-pilot hadn't sucked the flaps up from fifty-percent or one-hundred percent to zero. The speed at which the aircraft will stall increases, and it then takes more speed to keep from stalling. They stalled, and that was that. During an approach into Sparrevohn, you would fly the approach at fifty-percent flaps, and once you were committed to land, you would select one-hundred percent flaps. Where the flaps were at the beginning of the go-around was not known, but they were found to be at zero at the crash site. Mad Dog may have called for "Flaps" or "Flaps fifty." Either way the co-pilot moved the lever to zero.

The co-pilot had documented flap management deficiencies. There were only three flap setting on the Herk. Zero for flight, fifty percent for takeoff and landing and one-hundred percent for landing. We're not talking brain surgery here. Seven people were killed that day: the captain, co-pilot, navigator, flight engineer, load master and two passengers. The entire crew and aircraft were lost for one miss-position of the flap lever.

"Aviation in itself is not inherently dangerous. But to an even greater degree than the sea, it is terribly unforgiving of any carelessness, incapacity or neglect."Captain A. G. Lamplugh

Now MAC (not to be confused with my friend Mac), descended on us like a swarm of locusts. They checked every record and interviewed staff and pilots. Mad Dog had confided in me only a few weeks before the crash. He told me he wasn't getting enough "stick time," and he needed to stay current, just like any other pilot. MAC fired the safety team because there was an accident. So, obviously, the team hadn't done their job. *Right?* Bullshit. MAC was there for about two weeks. Then, as quickly as they arrived, they were gone. Months later, their report was released and said, "Currency of the pilots was *not* a contributing factor in the crash." Like cats burying crap.

Memorial Service

They had a beautiful memorial service for Mad Dog and his crew at the base chapel. It deeply affected me. The stained glass windows and the message the priest gave were nothing short of inspirational. The Dog was Irish, and we celebrated his passage with an Irish Wake. The party lasted late into the morning.

"And we both know what memories can bring. They bring diamonds and rust." *Joan Baez*

About a month after the memorial service, I accepted Jesus Christ as my Lord and Savior. Though many would question that conversion, it would take over thirteen years to be complete. For me it was a process.

Additional Duty

All pilots who flew had additional duties and office jobs. Days not flying were spent in the squadron doing something. Shortly after I arrived, I was assigned to be a Pilot Crew Scheduler. It was a great job. It was like playing third base in baseball, all the hot balls were hit to you. It was where all the action was. – multitasking on steroids. Talk about an adrenaline rush! *Wow!* I did that job for about three-and-a-half years.

Drinking

Note: There are three types of drinkers: social, problem and alcoholics. As it was explained to me in one of my classes on substance abuse. A social drinker, if handed a glass of wine with a fly in it, will politely decline and return the drink. If you hand the same drink to a problem drinker, they will say, "There's a fly in my drink." Then, they will remove the fly and consume their drink. In the case of an alcoholic, they will remove the fly, squeeze all the alcohol out of it and then consume the drink and after eat the fly.

I had digressed from being a social drinker, both figuratively and literally, to that of a problem drinker.

On New Year's Eve 1978, I got myself really drunk at the Officer's Club. I embarrassed my wife and myself. I behaved like a real asshole, not unlike a fighter pilot. I had to go to the bathroom, and as I was washing up, I looked in the mirror and saw my first and last alcohol-induced hallucination. There in the mirror was my father, and he winked at me. That was that. We left the club about ten minutes prior to midnight. My wife was so disgusted with me that she wouldn't talk. She drove home. Good idea – I was in no condition to drive.

The next day, January 1st 1979, I woke up with a terrible hangover. *Ya think?* My wife was barely speaking to me. I said to her, "I acted like a real jerk last night, didn't I?" She said, "Yes you did." I replied, "I don't think I'm a jerk." She said, "You're not." Then I said, "I think I should stop drinking." To which she answered, "I think that would be a good idea." I haven't had a drop of alcohol since. I didn't tell her about the hallucination until many years later. So, for those who knew me after and didn't understand why I wouldn't drink, now you know. All I had to do was reach back into my memory and remember my first childhood recollection. I had control over my hand and my destiny. Quitting drinking was easy. Other things in my life not so much so.

Tales of Flight

Pilots love to tell stories. My daughter, hearing these stories all of her life, developed an unnatural fear of flying. I always wondered why? In later years, she would fly the world.

While I was at Elmendorf, the C-130 community had a ground safety incident at McChord AFB, Washington. When you land a C-130, you pull the throttles back, then up and over a notch to put the props into reverse. It helps slow the aircraft without the use of brakes. Normally, you let the aircraft slow some with props in reverse then apply brakes as you slow down. It increases the life span of the brakes by not heating them up as much.

As the aircraft commander was putting the props into reverse, one of the outboard throttle cables broke. That meant that, the aircraft was uncontrollable. Three props were in reverse and one going full throttle forward. They did a couple of ground loops, exited the runway and came to a stop in the infield, between the runways. The dirt and mud helped to stop the plane. The safety board found the broken cable and exonerated the entire crew. They had done nothing wrong. We, of course, would read the safety reports. They were educational and gave insight into flying. If they had made a mistake, perhaps we could learn from it. Normally, they didn't give the crew members names right away. After the incident, they did. While reviewing the report, one of the old heads said, "Oh crap! I know the captain –J. Hummer. Couldn't happen to a nicer guy.

He's a snake in the grass. If you ever see him walking down the sidewalk, cross the street."

Pilots seldom tell you about taking off from Elmendorf AFB in the darkest of winter. Early in the morning, fog and visibility made it barely good enough to be legal to takeoff. We accelerated down the runway, building speed, lifting into the sky, and then had the visibility go completely blank. It was like being on the inside of a cotton ball. Thank heaven for instruments. We climbed, and at about one-thousand feet above the ground, broke through the clouds to a bright beautiful sky – you could see forever. The sun came up on the right side of the aircraft, and then, looking to my left I could see the rays bouncing, reflecting, dancing on Mount McKinley, and going in all directions. The reds, yellows, blues, greens and other colors were beyond description – not just a sunrise but a dawning, an awakening. It was a picture that is forever etched into my memory. Pilots will seldom tell stories like that.

When pilots do tell stories, they start with, "There I was." I will tell you about two of such flying experiences in Alaska. The first, not of my doing, and the second, entirely on me.

The first happened when I was a seasoned Captain. I knew my profession, and I was a good stick. I flew the airplane as well as anyone.

So, There I was…It was a joint Air Force/Army exercise. It was the Army's annual review – a huge deal for them. Our job was to support them in the movement of personnel and equipment. We were all gathered together in the briefing room. The door was closed and then locked. The first thing that happens in these briefings is the safety officer gets up and makes the following proclamation, "Safety is paramount. Nothing, either in the interest of training or expedience will compromise safety (paraphrasing)." The briefing officer would then give all the details of the flights. Then, pilots would go to *"Hack the Mission."* which means doing whatever you can to get the job done.

We were taking off from Elmendorf, middle of the winter and the weather was for crap. In these stories, the weather is normally the culprit. The winds were howling on the ground with gusts that shook the aircraft, rocking it from side to side. It was going to be a bad night for flying, and I knew it. But, *hack the mission.*

Our cargo that night was "Rolling Stock" – jeeps and trailers. The load master tied them down with chains, a hook at one end and a clevis at the other. He put his handiwork together, and secured the load. He did everything "by the book." He did nothing wrong. No fault goes to him. None.

We got everything loaded, and we were ready to go. Another C-130 took off about five minutes ahead of us. Then, it was our turn. I pushed the throttles up to full take-off power setting, released the brakes, and we were on our way. I had to fight the aircraft to keep it on centerline. The winds were buffeting us very hard and with gusts. As soon as I would make a correction, the wind would either increase or decrease, causing me to make constant changes to my corrections. When we lifted off, the aircraft immediately yawed about thirty-degrees to the left. I held it under control, but it was an incredible effort. We got to about twelve-hundred feet above the ground. The aircraft felt like it had been hit with a large hunk of concrete, weighing tons. It repeatedly struck the aircraft with such force. The aircraft was violently moved about. My readings in the cockpit were as follows: Airspeed, plus or minus forty knots; Altitude, plus or minus four-hundred feet; and Heading, plus or minus forty degrees. It was a forties kind of night. I was no longer in control of the plane, the turbulence was.

Most people who have ridden in a civilian aircraft think their lives are in danger when they hit a few bumps in the air. More often than not, it is light to moderate chop. Sometimes, it may be as bad as moderate turbulence. All aircraft, civilian or military, are not allowed to fly into areas of known or suspected severe or extreme turbulence. In severe turbulence, you lose control of the airplane. In extreme, parts of the aircraft can start falling off. We were in severe to extreme turbulence. The FAA (Federal Aviation Administration) defines, severe and extreme turbulence a follows:

Severe: This will cause changes in the accelerometer reading of greater than 1g at aircraft's center of gravity. Large, abrupt changes in altitude and/or attitude. It usually causes large variations in indicated airspeed. Aircraft may be momentarily out of control. Extreme: Turbulence in which the aircraft is violently tossed about and is practically impossible to control.

The higher we climbed, the worse the problem became. The rolling stock in the back began to pop its chains. The suspension on the equipment was so compressed during the violence, that it removed all the tension on the chain and the chain hooks started falling off. First one, then the others. This was a very bad situation. The rolling stock was now loose in the cargo compartment. We and the equipment were being tossed around like a rag doll. There are a lot of systems in the back of an aircraft: hydraulic, pneumatic, electrical, etc. You don't want a flying piece of equipment to hit any of them. With velocity, momentum and mass in action, one of the trailers came loose, jumped, and positioned itself on top of the right side rails about six-to-eight-inches above the normal flooring and rested against the side of the airplane. It did not go through. The load master was now calling for help. We also carried very wide nylon straps on the plane. They have a hook on one end and a winching device on the other. The load master and navigator in the back were throwing the straps over the top of the equipment and securing it as fast as they could. They got the load secured and then used every available strap on board. This, while the aircraft was in fact in and out of control.

I would tell people later, "Fail both of my engines, give me complete electrical and hydraulic failure, and there is an excellent chance I will get you on the ground safely. But if I lose my flight controls, the ability for me to tell the airplane where to go, then I'm just another passenger riding with you to the scene of the crash."

Our initial cleared altitude (as high as you are allowed to go), by ATC (Air Traffic Control), was five thousand feet. I had a handful of a very angry bull. I tried to level at three thousand feet. We were still getting the stuffing knocked out of us. I declared an in-flight emergency with ATC, "Loose cargo in the cargo bay." I also, reported the severe turbulence to ATC. I was going to return to base. I had read the FAA's book on turbulence, and I knew the difference between moderate, severe and extreme. I had the co-pilot call the weather shop on base to report the severe turbulence. They told us to, "Standby." Standby, my ass. All these transmissions were going out over the radios. The aircraft which had taken off before us called on operations frequency and told me the weather was fine. He claimed that at about five thousand it gets better. *Really?* He had gone through this crap and didn't give anyone a pilot report as required by Federal Aviation Rules. Screw the safety briefing. Screw the other pilots and crews. Hack the mission at all costs. I continued to get "standbys" from the weather shop. Screw that. I barely kept the aircraft together and under control, and they're telling me to standby? Now, in addition to having gotten the stuffing knocked out of us by the turbulence, I was pissed.

I got the aircraft on downwind and then finally on final. I had to cross a body of water and the problem got worse for a while. At about eight hundred feet, I had regained enough control to land. I parked the aircraft and asked for crew transportation. They said, "It is on the way and the group commander wants to see and talk to you." I walked in and the commander asked, "Just who in the hell do you think you are bringing this operation to a halt?" Then, he proceeded to give me a royal ass-chewing. Because of me, the whole operation was cancelled. We hadn't supported the mission.

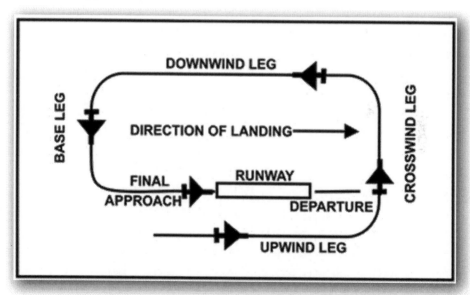

That night, shortly thereafter, two commercial airliners, Delta and Western tried to fly into the Anchorage bowl. At about five thousand feet, above the ground, they reported severe turbulence and diverted to Fairbanks. Anchorage

International Airport closed the field to any further air traffic. Diversions went on all night and into the morning. Did I then get called in to be thanked for my excellent airmanship? Hell no! So much for air safety.

I upgraded to Instructor Pilot in 1980. Once again in Little Rock. My evaluator, Captain Mike-Mike, wrote in my assessment what an outstanding job I had done on all the air work. The thing about being an Instructor Pilot is that your flying skills are at the best that they will ever be. You can now fly the airplane like no one else ever and instruct at the same time. It makes you feel ten-feet tall and bulletproof.

The second incident happened after I had been upgraded to Instructor. I got to do a lot of neat stuff. I became the Strip-Check-Instructor-Pilot for Cape Romanzof, a patch of ground cut out of the side of a mountain with cliffs on three sides and a hill on the other. At the end of the airstrip was a mountain climbing high above. A go-around was not an option. A good approach and landing in the zone was paramount. Suffice it to say, I was always very alert during these training flights. Other neat things included carrying some VIP's. A certain U.S. Congressman from the state of Arizona was a pleasant enough chap. He came up to the flight deck and said, "Don't ***k this up." *Oh, thank you, Sir. May I have another?* It's not just fighter pilots who are assholes.

Another thing I got to do was air shows. I was to perform two, one at Elmendorf on Saturday and the other at Allen Army Air Field in Fairbanks on Sunday. The demonstration would begin with me doing a random steep approach. I was to come in very high above the field, do a spiraling three-hundred-and-sixty-degree descending turn, followed by a two-hundred-and-seventy-degree descending teardrop turn to align myself with the runway. It was kind of like a corkscrew. Then, I was to land in the *zone*. The zone began one hundred feet from the end of the runway and extended to five-hundred feet from the end. The total zone was four-hundred feet long. The daddy rabbit of the show (the person in charge) was an Air Force Lt. Col and a fighter pilot. He asked me where I was going to land on the runway. I explained to him what the zone was. He wasn't impressed. Then, I told him I could put it down on any spot he wanted, plus or minus ten feet, as long as the spot was within the four-hundred foot zone. That seemed to make him happy. BTW, I hit the spot.

After landing, we would do a maximum anti-skid braking demonstration, bringing the aircraft to a halt in a very short distance. Easy enough to do. We didn't have anything in the cargo bay. We were light. Then the load master would open the rear cargo ramp as we were coming to a stop. Once stopped, he would give me directions to back up the airplane. I would put the props in reverse, and it would back up. We went to the spot for takeoff, closing the rear ramp, then brought the aircraft to a halt. I ran the power up to maximum takeoff with the brakes set, then jumped off the brakes, accelerated down the runway and in a very short distance, we were airborne. Okay, not only me, but my commander, the crew, my fellow pilots, all thought it was a ten – a perfect score – and it was.

That night, we flew to Fairbanks. The next morning, Sunday, we would do our show. The weather was against us, of course. We had to start our approach at a lower altitude. We started our spiraling descent, but in my teardrop turn I overshot and went past the centerline of the runway. It was a left hand turn, so as to be on my side of the aircraft. I saw the runway going behind me and to my left. I started pulling and banking to get back on center line. The bush pilots would call this a Moose Hunter's Stall. The pilot/hunter would see the moose and try to return to where it was, stall the aircraft and likely die. I used all my pilot skills to get us into this position. It was a total screw up on my part.

"*A superior pilot uses his superior judgment to avoid situations which require the use of his superior skills.*" ~ *Frank Borman Apollo 8*

All of a sudden, I noticed the aircraft got really quiet. The C-130 is never quiet. I looked down and saw what was happening and glanced at the airspeed indicator. It read fifty-seven knots. Because you can't stall a Zero G aircraft, I simultaneously pushed the throttles to full maximum, pushed the yoke full forward, turned the yoke to the right to get the right high wing down and pushed as hard as I could on right rudder pedal to get the airplane level and out of the stall. Nothing worked. Right before we were about to crash and burn, I thought to myself, "*Oh God*, not my crew." It might have been the first unselfish act I ever did in my life. If you will remember from the Sprite crash, when I thought, "Oh God, *I* could die," my thoughts were only about me. This time, I only thought of others and not of myself at all. It was my responsibility to keep them safe, to get them into the air and then back on the ground, all in one piece. At the very moment I said my prayer to God, the aircraft started to fly again. I recovered the aircraft and continued to land. We were out of the zone. Forget about a spot. When we were backing up, the airplane got cocked. It didn't go back in a straight line like we planned. We had to abruptly end that maneuver. When I put the brakes on the nose of the aircraft looked like it bowed down. The announcer said it was part of the show. We did our short field takeoff. It was a quiet flight back to Elmendorf. Everyone knew. On a scale of one to ten, it didn't even garnish a one. I went back later and looked in the books. There is no way a C-130 will fly at fifty-seven knots.

"Never quit. Never give up. Fly it to the end." Chuck Aaron, Aerobatic Helicopter pilot

I was no longer "Ten Feet Tall" nor "Bulletproof", but I had forged a covenant with God. From that moment on, I knew that anyone put under my protection in the aircraft would never be harmed. I flew for thirty-two years. In that time, no one got hurt, nothing got bent, and I never had to call the FAA and explain myself.

I got back to the squadron the next day, and I expected the squadron commander would give me the royal ass-chewing I deserved and more. I opened the door. He was just inside the doorway about ten feet away. He saw me and came over with a huge grin on his face and gave me a handshake. He said, "Congratulations, I saw the airshow here, and it was *outstanding*. And I understand the one in Fairbanks went as well." I said, "Well, the one in Fairbanks didn't go nearly as well as here." He said, "Everyone was happy and I'm happy." *Hack the mission right?!* I nearly killed myself and my crew for no damned good reason.

Leaving

I received a call one day from the Military Personnel Center asking if I was planning on making a career of the Air Force. By now, I had spent nearly five years in Alaska. I told him I was and he said, "Well, you can't do it all in Alaska." He gave me a choice of two duty assignments, Pope or Little Rock, AFB. I chose Little Rock. I had spent a lot of time there training over the years.

Personnel explained to me about the training squadrons needing instructor pilots. If I would agree to go to one of the three training squadrons, I would be given a designation (Code 51) that would guarantee a follow-on assignment. If my desired assignment was available, and I qualified, I would be first in line to get it. The problem with talking with someone over the phone is you can't tell if their lips are moving or not.

That was in mid-July 1981. I was to leave Anchorage, which had become my home. I talked with my commander as I was out processing. I said, "This is the first time I've ever had a reassignment of any significance. I have moved before but not from a flying squadron to a flying squadron. I don't really know how these things are done. You know me here, know what I can do etc. Could you write a letter of introduction to my new squadron commander?" He said, "I don't know your new squadron commander, but I do know the *Wing Commander* very well. I will send him a letter for you." The Wing Commander is the senior officer on the base. Everyone works for him. I thanked my squadron commander as I left Elmendorf.

Road Trip

We sold our cars in Alaska. I had purchased another Porsche in 1980. A 1976 Porsche 912E (I still have the car). I stored it in Portland for a year awaiting my return from Alaska. We bought a brand new VW Scirocco and took delivery of it in Portland. We set out on a cross country road trip from Portland to Little Rock, Arkansas. We purchased two CB radios so we could communicate with each other on the road. We pulled into Little Rock having had very few issues on route.

My New Assignment

We checked in on base, did all the in-processing and I was off to my new squadron — the basic school. I would be training brand newbies right from pilot training and captain upgrades. I was excited about it. I got to my squadron, met a few people, and then I saw Mr. Red Pants, from SOS. He was Chief of Standardization and Evaluations – the "Red Pants" of any flying squadron. The squadron had just completed an evaluation from MAC, which was a huge thing. Mr. Red Pants was in charge of it all, and they did extremely well. The Commander was fond of him.

A week passed, and I asked to say hello to the Commander. You know, "Hi. I'm me and happy to be here." I went in with the Chief Pilot. The Commander was very stern. He told me the way things were going to be. After we left, the Chief Pilot said, "Damn, What was that all about? It almost sounded like an ass-chewing." I said, "I don't know." Of course I did. Another week or so passed, and the Commander's attitude changed toward me a lot. Obviously, the letter my Commander in Alaska wrote and sent to the Wing Command had worked its way down to my new Commander's desk. Mr. Red Pants was telling him one thing in one ear, and the Wing Commander was telling him something else in the other. I never read the letter, but I can assume it was warm and fuzzy.

I set about training new pilots on how to fly the Herk. It was fun to see the lights turn on as the students figured out systems and how to fly. Most had a good attitude. A few thought they should be flying fighters. Turns out, most of the time, those ones were the worst sticks.

The students wrote evaluations on the instructors. By then, the Commander's smile broadened when he saw me in the hall. One day, the Commander came to me and said, "Todd, we're going to have our first female C-130 pilot go through the program. I'm choosing you to be her instructor." Cool enough. She had made it through pilot training, and she was fully qualified to be there. I didn't care that she needed to squat to pee. She was a good stick and passed with flying colors. Her name was "Rocky."

Another female pilot was having trouble flying the plane. The Commander told me that he was going to change instructors, and I would train her. Fine with me. I talked with her previous instructor to find out what was going on. He said, "She can't fly the airplane, and she shouldn't be taking a pilot slot that should go to a man." Well okay then, I found out what half the problem was right there. I met her, and she knew her stuff. She had been studying. I thought, okay, that's not a problem. Then, I did a personal assessment of her physical stature. She should never have been assigned to the C-130. She was too short and small.

We got in the cockpit the first day and I noticed right off the bat what the problem was. She couldn't reach the rudder pedals. She had to get the seat up high to be able to see over the glare shield, and that put her further away from the pedals. She had the seat as far forward as it would go and the pedals as close to her as they get. She still had trouble using them to get full rudder deflection. I got a parachute block and put it between her and the back of the chair. This, to get her closer to the flight controls. It worked. We came up with a better solution for ride two.

The other problem was that she was scared to death that she might fail. Her first instructor had been yelling at her the whole time, and she was a bundle of nerves. Instead of yelling at her, I laughed when she screwed up. I told her what she had done wrong and how to fix it. She relaxed and passed her check ride. She wrote an evaluation on her two instructors. I fared extremely well, the other instructor, not so much so.

I was assigned to teach a fighter pilot how to fly the Herk. He was going to be a Squadron Commander at a C-130 unit and had never flown the Herk before. He was a VIP, and I noticed he didn't have a designated parking spot. So, I got him one. He was a good fighter pilot, but big airplanes fly differently. The Herk wasn't a fighter after all, but he learned enough and passed. He then wrote an incredible evaluation for me. Not only was I a great instructor, but he wanted me to come to work for him in his new squadron. By now, my stock with the Commander was in the stratosphere.

One day, I was to fly with Lt. Col. Don. He was the Commander of the Ground and Instructor school – the one that teaches instructors how to instruct. We went to the flight line, checked out the airplane, and then went to base operations. When you were on the flight line, you had to wear a flight line badge, but you were not supposed to wear it off the flight line. Just one of those things. I noticed he still had his badge on. I heard two people behind me talking on the phone to the IG (Inspector General). They would notice things like that and write a report on you. I got between Lt. Col. Don and the IG team and said, "Sir, you still have your line badge on and the guys behind me are from the IG." He removed his badge and asked, "How do you know they are from the IG?" I said,

"I overheard them talking on the phone." My stock was rising with him. We went out and flew a five-hour navigational training mission. We talked and got along well. I said, "I'd like to come work for you." He said, "I would love to have you as an academics instructor." I replied, "No Sir, I would like to go to the Instructor School." His mouth and jaw tightened. I knew I had hit a nerve of some sort. He said sternly, "If you do come to work for me in the instructor school, I will not allow an independent and autonomous instructor working for me. You would be part of my squadron. Do you understand me?" I replied, "That would not be a problem, Sir."

The training mission was on a Saturday. He told me, "I will wait an appropriate amount of time and then put in a by-name request for you." I said, "Okay, thank you, Sir." Monday morning, I received notification I was getting a new assignment. I was going to the Instructor School. My Commander hated to see me go but wrote me an exceptional Officer's Evaluation Report.

The Instructor School

The Instructor School was an elite group of seven pilots who taught all the C-130 pilots in the world how to instruct. When I arrived at the school, it was to a cold welcome. It seems Lt. Col. Don had gone to the Instructor School a few weeks earlier. He had chewed their collective asses out, but good. In part, he said, "I will not allow nor will I accept an independent and autonomous Instructor School you're part of my squadron, and you work for me."

Oh, shit! I had just moved from a nice cushy job and found myself in a hornets nest. I was handpicked by Lt. Col. Don, so obvious I was his *spy*. What else could I be? I was not Don's spy, but it's hard to change people's mind when they're already made up. The next eighteen months at Little Rock were not as pleasant as the one's before.

The Combined Federal Campaign

Lt. Col. Don called me to his office one day and said, "Todd, you need to get your name out there. No one knows who you are. The Combined Federal Campaign is starting in a couple of weeks, and I want you to be the coordinator for the base. Are you interested?" At times like this, the only answer is, "Sir, yes, Sir." He talked with the Wing Commander that afternoon, and I had the job. The problem was, they had already promised the job to another pilot. *Oops.* Once again, Lt. Col. Don was trying to help me and had taken the job from another pilot. Oh boy. I took the bull by the horns and went at the assignment with full gusto.

There were, of course, issues along the way. The entire base had about forty units, and I had to coordinate with all of them. There were three training squadrons on base: The Basic School, where I came from, the Combat Training Squadron, and the Academic/Instructor Squadron. I assembled everyone in a hanger and told them what needed to be done and by when. Each week, they were to give me a status report on how close they were to achieving their goal. During the first week, the Basic and Instructor Squadrons did as told. However, the Combat Squadron didn't turn in their status report. Each week, I had to brief the Wing Commander and the Command Staff on our progress. I put the numbers up on an overhead projector. The Basic and Instructor Squadrons had one-hundred percent of their goal the first week. The Combat School Squadron had zero. The Wing Commander made reference to it. The Commander of the Combat School had been embarrassed. He went back to his squadron and chewed his Operations Officer a new asshole. It was part of his job to see that things like this got done. His name was Lt. Col. Bob. By the way, the pilot who had been promised the base campaign coordinator position was the Combat Training Squadron's Action Officer. It was his job to get the report to me.

We attained one-hundred-and-twenty-six percent of our goal. The Wing Commander called me to his office and congratulated me. He was a very happy camper indeed. I don't think I was on the Combat Training Squadron's Christmas card list that year. I was in Base Operations about three months later and a handful of the top Command Staff were there. They all knew my name, came over to me and chatted me up.

Half way through my time at the Instructor School, we got a new commander. Lt. Col. Don left for Europe, and his replacement was Lt. Col. Bob from the Combat Training School – the same one who had his ass chewed out for the campaign and thought it was because of me and not the Action Officer in his squadron. My stock fell to a new low. My last six months at the Instructor School were miserable. Oh well, at least the Wing Commander still liked me. My additional duty at the Instructor School was Pilot Scheduler, but this time it was at the wing level.

Promotion

I wanted to get promoted to Major. There were a number of requirements. First, I would have to complete Air Command and Staff – one of three Service School in the Air Force. I did so by seminar. Second, I needed a Master's Degree. More often times than not, these were done in your spare time. I looked at the list of Master's programs available on base. I didn't want to get an MBA. I had enough business classes in college for that. Then, in front of my eyes, was a Master's Degree in Psychology. Psychology was one of the core classes I needed twelve hours of when I was in college. I had gotten twenty-four hours in that discipline, all A's. Psychology was a subject that, to me, was just common sense. I got it.

I enrolled in the program. I had straight A's until the very last class. I was assigned to go to Headquarters Pacific with a report date of December 1984. I had to go to a school at Wright Patterson, AFB, conflicting with my last Masters class. I would have to miss half of the term. I went to the professor and told him the circumstances. He said, "Then don't bother to take my class." I reminded him that the school had promised to be flexible with us because of our military service. I didn't see his actions as being flexible. He *very* reluctantly agreed. The class had three graded items, two tests and a writing assignment. I had a friend in the class and she shared all of her lecture notes and what she could remember from the class. After my return from Wright Patterson the first test was in less than a week. I studied and got a B plus. On the paper and final test I got A's. Two A's and one high B an A makes, right? Not so fast. He gave me a B.

That B haunted me for years. I wanted to get a 4.0 GPA to prove to myself and anyone else who might care that I was a "Slow Learner" no more. I went to school four nights a week and finished my Master's Program in eighteen months. I graduated with a 3.95 cumulative GPA. Now I look back on it and any way you cut it that's not too shabby.

A new assignment

By the time it came to take my new assignment, the Code 51 was a thing of the past and didn't apply to me. I had not requested Hawaii as a duty station and I didn't really want to go. One man's treasure, is another man's trash. Thank you MPC (Military Personnel Center).

For my new assignment I had to drive cross country to the West Coast to put my car on a boat. We sold the VW, and put the Orange Porsche in storage again. This time for three years. I stored it with my buddy, Mac. During my time in Arkansas I found and purchased a white 1969 Porsche 912. I took that one with me to Hawaii. I now had two Porsche's.

I arrived in Hawaii three months before my wife did. We were trying to sell a house in North Little Rock without a lot of luck. Finally, just as she was preparing to come join me, she sold the house.

My wife and I had tried very successfully not to have any babies in the first nine years of our marriage. Then, we decided to have children and weren't being successful. She would stand on her head, eat special diets, take her temperature, and say, "It's time, Bubba. We're going to the back room." She would grab me by my ear and pull me to the bedroom. I would cry the whole way, "Oh, no! Not that Not that, again." Well, it might not have happened exactly like that, but it's my story. I'll tell it the way I want. Besides, it reads better this way. She got used to the laid-back, slower life style of the islands. She was so relaxed that she got pregnant twice while we were there. I still had some PTSD and stayed on base a lot.

Staff Job

At the school I attended at Wright Patterson AFB, I was to become an Action Officer for U. S. Military Assistance and Foreign Military Sales. Yes, I was now a gun runner for the mob.

I had very limited prior staff experience, but I spun up to speed in a short time. I would move paper from the left side of my desk to the right. I also got to brief general officers and their staff. I am an extrovert, so getting up in front of a group of people and talking was not a problem for me. I had a captive audience. I loved it, and it was fun.

The Trip

CincPacAF is a four-star general officer position. It is the highest rank in the Military, except during wartime when they can (rarely) become a five-star. General Bob was a gentleman of the first order. I liked working for him. He had a good worldview, and from where he sat, he could see the big picture. He was in charge of all Air Force air assets in the Pacific. He wanted to visit his domain. We were going to the Philippines, Singapore, Thailand, Okinawa and Japan. My job was to make sure it happened. I had to write a "Trip Book" explaining each country, U. S. and host country inventories of air assets, and arrange meetings with embassies, ambassadors and heads of U. S. commands. It was a big deal. No, not big. Huge!

We set out with seven stars on board. The four-star General Bob, the newly crowned two-star General Tom, and my boss in Plans, the one-star General Dan. The first two legs of the trips were mostly uneventful. Then, we arrived in Thailand. We spent time in Bangkok, visiting the Joint U. S. Military Advisor Group Thailand and the Commander-in-Chief of the Royal Thai Air Force. He was the top-ranking general officer for the Thai Air Force. The Thai General decided he wanted us to join him on a trip to Chiang Mai, Thailand, up north and in the mountains. General Bob said, "That won't be a problem. Will it, Major Howe?" I replied, "Oh, no, Sir. No problem at all." All I would have to do is completely change all of the itineraries and appointments for the remainder of the trip. Not a problem at all, with our limited ability to communicate and all.

We proceeded to Chiang Mai. The Thai General reserved a second floor room at a restaurant and bar. The only people on the first floor were security, and there were a lot of them. We went upstairs and had a nice dinner, but the party started to lag. The Generals were beginning to look a little uncomfortable. So, being the trouble-maker I always was, I got up from my table and went to another with more people. I put my arms over their shoulders and said, "Hey, this party is beginning to drag. Let's sing 'You've Lost That Loving Feeling' to the Thai Chiefs wife." General Dan was watching every move I made. You could see the terror in his eyes. That look of fear, as he thought, *Oh, no! Is he going to embarrass me?* The group I conspired with, after having had a drink or two, decided that was a most excellent idea. We got up and went to the center of the room. General Dan looked like he was going to have a stroke at any moment. I announced that we were going to dedicate a song to the Thai General's wife. General Dan looked like he had just wet his pants. Then we started singing, "Baby you've lost that loving feeling — oh, that loving feeling. Bring back that loving feeling, cause it's gone, gone. gone, and I can't go on. Whoa!" It was only a couple of verses, but it was the spark. General Bob got up from his chair, came over to our group, put his arm over my shoulder and said, "That was great, Todd! Now what?" *Oh, crap!* I thought. *I'm a one-trick pony*. Still, we came up with some other ideas and put on a show for all of them. After that, the party was rocking. The remainder of the trip was uneventful. General Dan seemed to have calmed down a little.

I was initially hired by Lt. Col. Gary. A year after I arrived, he decided he wasn't making enough progress where he was, so he jumped ship to another staff job. My new boss was Lt. Col. J. Hummer. He was a C-130 pilot. There were five pilots in the shop: two wanted to return to flying and the other three did not. I had already formed an opinion of Hummer, but he was now my immediate supervisor. I asked him one day why he didn't want to fly anymore. He said, "Because the Herk tried to kill me. I was landing at McChord one day, and an outboard throttle cable broke. We did a number of three-hundred-and-sixty degrees turns before the aircraft stopped in the in-field." *Oh, my God! It was him!* This was the "Snake in the Grass" I had been warned about years ago, and now, I was working for him. The assessment by the pilot in Alaska was accurate.

Evaluations

The Air Force was always changing the way they did their evaluation system for promotion. While I was in Hawaii they were going through what was nicknamed "Star Wars." General officers had stars for their rank, and the higher the level of General, the more stars. Your job was to get your evaluation to have the most number of stars. In three years, you would have three evaluations. If you had a one-star general's endorsement each year you would have a total of three stars. But if just one of the three evaluations were a four star you would double your three stars with six. The first year I was in Hawaii I got a one-star endorsement.

The second year, I had flown with CincPacAF and had twenty-three letters of appreciation. Four came from the Chiefs of Staff of their respective Air Forces in Australia, Thailand, Singapore and the Philippians. I was told my evaluation was going to go to the four-star, and it should have. I got a one-star endorsement. I worked with a Major from fighters who had been passed over for promotion the year before. Our supervisor J. Hummer decided to save his career and get him a four-star endorsement. The number of four-star endorsements were limited. That four-star endorsement should have been mine. At that point, I had a very sour taste in my mouth for both the Air Force and the fighter pilot community. After that, I was done with the Air Force. All I wanted to do was put in twenty years, retire and fly for the airlines. My last year, I also got a one-star. Three stars in all. Remember, the CINC has four stars.

Little Baby Girl (LBG)

My wife came into the living room one night, nine-and-half-months pregnant and said, "I think my water broke." I asked, "When do you think you'll know for sure?" She disappeared into the bathroom, and, emerged again, said, "It has." *What?* Oh, shit! She's having a baby. She said, "I'm having contractions." I asked, "How far apart?" She said, "Four minutes." I thought of all the Lamaze classes we had taken and remembered that four minutes meant something important. All that time in Vietnam, all the excitement I had flying airplanes were nothing to prepare me for this. At that point, I was like "Donald Duck on the good ship lollipop." I jumped up, grabbed the "go bag", and we hustled off to Tripler Army Hospital. I went to the wrong entrance, and I didn't see any way to get to the door other than climbing down a hillside. So, we did. We were at the Emergency Room. The hospital staff said, "It isn't an emergency. She is only having a baby. She needs to go to maternity." *Okay, where is it?* They gave us directions, and away we went. We arrived, and realized we shouldn't have been in such a hurry. She was in labor for the next twenty hours.

After twenty hours, it was time to take her to the delivery room. The nurse said, "There is a problem, and she might have to have an emergency C-Section."

If so, I wouldn't be able to be in the delivery room with her. Then, they called in the pro. He stuck his hands up inside my wife, moved some things around, and said, "Push!" I was supposed to help, but all I heard was this very weak and faint voice ask, "Push?" She pushed for a long time, and finally, I began to see a golf ball coming out of my wife. Then, it became a softball, and I thought, *damn, woman.* When they removed the "Cone head", it was the size of a football.

LBG arrived with her eyes wide open. They are still open to this day. I got to hold my newborn baby in my hands. The nurse said, "Ten fingers and ten toes. She's good to go."

And do you know what they did next? They gave this little bundle of life to us and sent us home. How crazy is that? She didn't come with an operating manual. There weren't any instructions. My wife got pregnant a second time in Hawaii. This time, it was an LBG (Little Baby Guy), but he wouldn't be born there.

Military Personnel Center One, Todd Won!

I was working at my staff job at Hickam AFB. It was early February 1987 or so, and I called the Personnel Center. They were also known as "Those Flesh-Peddling, Slave-Trading Bastards." After my experience with them and the Code 51, I wanted to know what they had in mind for me. They said, "Return to Little Rock, back to the school house." That's where I had come from, and I knew it would be a dead end. I said, "No, I can extend here in Hawaii I'm doing a good job, and they'll sign off on it." He replied, "Okay, then do it." So, I extended for an additional six months. At that point, in place of leaving in December 1987, I would leave the following June 1988. In October, Personnel called me back. They said, "We now have a critical pilot shortage." The way they treated people, I was not surprised. He said, "We need experience in C-130's. Anywhere you want to go." I said, "Well, if you need experience in C-130's, you must need it in other weapon systems (airplanes) too." He said, "Well, we need experience at the 89th." The 89th is the Presidential Unit Support Squadron. I wouldn't be flying the President but other VIP's. I said, "Okay, are you going to release me from C-130's to interview with the 89th?" They said, "Yes, we'll send you a message." I waited about three days and the message came. It said in bold letters, "RELEASED FROM C-130's to interview with the 89th."

The next thing I did was call the C-9 Nightingale equipment manager at MAC. MAC is a subordinate Major Command to MPC for personnel matters. It all follows a process. I asked, "Hey, how about a job with the C-9?" He asked who I was. I gave him all the information, and he looked at my records. He said, "There is no way you are going to get a C-9." Remember those times in ROTC? Never say, "Never."

> Note:Why the C-9? The McDonnell Douglas C-9 is a military version of the McDonnell Douglas DC-9 jet airliner. It was produced as the C-9A Nightingale for the U. S. Air Force. The C-9's were used for aeromedical evacuation, passenger transportation, and special missions. I wanted to get the C-9 assignment to better situate myself for being hired by the airlines.

The Air Force wants their pilots to fly but not too much, so as to allow the younger pilots to get some experience. The Air Force has what is called "gates." Within the first number of years, you have to fly so much. I think the gates were the seven, nine and eleven-year points. I'm not exactly sure, but I know there were three of them. The C-9 manager said, "You have met all your gates." Yeah, I already knew that. I had already satisfied all the requirements for all of my gates. I had flown enough. Then, he said, "Besides, you can't get released from C-130's." I told him, "I have a teletype massage in my hand releasing me from 130's." He looked at all my evaluation reports. They were all good, and he knew it. He said, "You have general officer endorsements on all your evaluations. You should be looking for a job at the Pentagon." I didn't tell him that I already had a two-star General preparing a by-name request for me to work at the Pentagon. Among other things, I didn't want to work there. What I also didn't tell him was that my release from C-130's was conditional. *Oops! My bad.* I'm sure it was just an oversight on my part.

He was still trying to convince me it would never happen. I was certain that it would. I asked if he could take my records to the C-9 Squadron Commander's

Office, so the Commander could have a look at them. He said, "I'm not going to waste my time going over there." I asked, "What is it, like a mile or two?" He said, "No, it is only two blocks." I was quiet at the other end of the line. Then I said, "You mean to tell me you won't even take my records two blocks?" I had shamed him. "Oh, all right," he said, "I'll do it." I thanked him. That was on a Tuesday. Thursday morning he called me back. He said, "I don't believe it. I do *not* believe it. The Commander said you are exactly what he's looking for. He has a number of young lieutenants and captains, but he doesn't have any field grade officers (Majors and above). He wants more maturity in the squadron. He also wants someone with staff experience." I was a Major and had been at a Major Command Headquarters. I had three years of staff experience. In my way of thinking, that was two-and-half years too many.

He said, "The Commander is going to ask for you with a by-name request." That meant he wasn't looking for just a body. He wanted *my* body. This was a good position to be in. I hoped the request would get there before the two-star general's request for me to go to the Pentagon. The General thought I wouldn't be available until June of 1988.

The C-9 Commander's request came in first. The C-9 manager coordinated my assignment with the C-130's community at MAC. The managers sent the request up to the generals, and they all signed off on it. Then, the managers at MAC called the Personnel Center and told them what was happening. I had temporary duty in the Philippines at the time, and I was talking to the C-9 manager. I was sure I could see and hear an explosion coming from San Antonio, Texas, home of the Personnel Center. They were PISSED. They finally saw what I had done. They were going to deny me the assignment, which they could have done, but the C-9's had already lost two pilot assignments that had gotten this far in the process. Besides, I had a by-name request. The C-9 community wasn't about to lose another battle. They were fighting hard for me. It was a conversation between two majors, one at MAC and one at the Personnel Center. The C-9 guy was a captain. He gave me a blow by blow report over the phone. My future was in their hands. They exchanged pleasantries all in a very loud and heated manner. MAC said, "If you can release him from C-130's for the 89th, then you can release him for C-9's." All of a sudden, the captain said, "Awesome." I thought that might be good, right? I asked, "What happened?" Then, the captain told me that MPC just said, "Fine, if he wants to ruin his career, let him." The Personnel Center released me, and I was going to C-9's.

I had talked with my wife about it earlier. There were a lot of "what ifs." I asked, "What if I got a C-9? What if they would not cancel my extension? What if we had to move in the middle of winter? What if they won't let you travel?" My wife was eight months pregnant, and we had a seventeen-month-old. A lot of what ifs. Finally, she said, "Enough with the 'what ifs.' Show me a set of orders."

Two days later, I received a call from personnel at PACAF saying they had an assignment for me to go to C-9's. Personnel asked, "You don't want that, do you?" PACAF was a fighter command, and everything was about fighters. I was only "on loan" from MAC, but I was still a MAC resource. He didn't understand that. It was outside his scope of reference. He kept saying, "I can get them cancelled if you want." I said, "No, I want the assignment." Finally, I convinced him, and he replied, "Okay. Come on down, and get your authorization to get orders printed."

Their office was three flights below mine and on the other side of the building – about half a city block away. I hung up the phone and went running down to his office. I arrived in his office and at his desk by the time he had just hung up the phone. He asked, "Major Howe?" I said, "Yes." He said, "I just hung up the phone." Again, I replied, "Yes." He restated, "I mean, I *just* hung up the phone." I said, "Yes, I was in a hurry." He had my assignment in his hand and the authorization to get orders printed and start our out-processing. I wanted that authorization in my hands.

I took the authorization form to the printing office and asked if I could have the orders printed by close of business. They said they would have them later that day. I picked up my packet of orders that afternoon. I hadn't told my wife anything about it yet. I wanted to have the orders in my hand. That afternoon, when she got home from work, I had a piece of paper between my thumb and forefinger. I was waiving it back and forth. It made a fluttering sound.

Her response was, "You have got to be kidding me, right? Here, let me see them." I showed her the orders. She still didn't believe it. She would. Someone was always looking out for me. Thank you again, Guardian Angel.

My wife had to get a waiver to fly because she was eight months pregnant. I went with her to the Flight Surgeon's Office. He cleared her to fly. Another hoop jumped through. We had dinner with some friends on Thanksgiving, and the next day, I put my wife, my daughter and my soon-to-be son on the plane. Everything dear to me in my life was on that airplane that day.

I couldn't leave until the first of December. My friend, Mac, was going to come out to Long Beach and help me drive one of my three cars to Illinois. The Toyota Tercel and the white car, my 1969 Porsche 912, were going to Long Beach. They would be waiting for us on my arrival. I had also purchased another 1969 Porsche 912 in Hawaii We called it the "Green Car", and it would be going to New Orleans later. That made three Porsches.

Note: There were three production runs in 1969 of the Porsche 912: 0001 to 1000, 1001 to 1500, and 1501 to 1850. Both of my 912's were from the third and final production run of the final production year. They were thirty-seven numbers apart. They were considered the best of the best 912's.

Porsches on parade: Orange 1976 912E, White 1969 912 and Green 1969 912.

Mac couldn't get the time off from work. I think if both Porsches had gone to Long Beach he might have found the time.

My father in-law, George, said, "If you need any help, call me." I did call him. We met at the airport in Los Angles — this, before cell phones. We arranged ground transport to the Long Beach Pier. I filled out all the appropriate paperwork, and we were on our way. Long Beach to Saint Louis in the winter. The trip was mostly on I-40.

It didn't get off to a great start. George wanted to stop and get some food, and I was trying to get us out of the dock area to find someplace where there was food. I couldn't find any. He got pissed. He turned around and started going back. I had to go back to get him and talk him down. We found a place to eat and were on our way. I was paying for all the food and lodging. George picked up the airfare. I tried to reimburse him, and he wouldn't have anything to do with it.

The first night we stayed at a nice hotel in Flagstaff, Arizona. It was a little loud though. Flagstaff is a college town, so they were having a party. It sounded like good clean fun, and it was over by midnight. The next day we departed for Albuquerque. We got there too early, so we decided to press on. We found some little rat-hole along the side of the road in a town called Tucumcari, New Mexico. George let me know that it was unacceptable housing, but we stayed the night anyway. He was right, and the next day, we stayed in a nice place outside the city limits of Oklahoma City, Oklahoma.

As we were leaving the next day, there was some construction. George and I almost ran into each other. It was our only close call on the entire trip. There was also a toll road issue. I had gotten through it, but he was delayed. I pulled over to the side of the road a little ways ahead of him. Then, I saw him pass me, going balls-to-the-wall, trying to catch up. He didn't realize that I was behind him. I got the Porsche up to speed and caught up to him in short order. I pulled in front and got him to slow down. We continued on.

Note: I had gotten the engine in the white car rebuilt in Hawaii and I was breaking it in during this trip. I would accelerate to 3000 RPM and then back to 2000 RPM. I did that until Oklahoma. Then, I took it up to 3500 RPM and after Springfield, Missouri up to 4000 RPM and so on. I sold the car 30,000 miles later, and it never used a drop of oil.

We stopped for some lunch, and George told me he didn't know where we were going. We were still on I-40. Every morning, we would plot out our strategies, but he didn't know the final destination point. I gave him the address in

Belleville, Illinois, but I had no idea where it was. Both he and I now had a piece of paper with an address, but we had no idea where we were going. Still, the address seemed to calm him down some. That night, we stayed in Springfield, Missouri. I calculated that we could leave in the morning and make Belleville by late afternoon or early dusk. Of course, I was talking with my wife every day. When we got close, I asked her to give me some local directions. She came up with directions — some that even worked! We arrived at the correct apartment with only one missed approach. When we got inside, my eighteen-month-old daughter saw me. She fell to the floor, bowing down and worshiping me. She hadn't seen me for a while. I had always been there for her, and she was afraid I had gone Missing-in-Action. I picked her up, held her and hugged her. She didn't want to let go. Unfortunately, that would change in later life.

Settling In

George and I had gotten in later than I wanted, but we could still see. The next day, we took him to the airport in Saint Louis and said our goodbyes. George and I were still talking, which was a good sign, I think. My first couple of days in Belleville were spent buying winter clothes and getting situated. Finally, I got my bearings. Then, we found a realtor. She was the wife of a Lt. Col. Rick, who was also stationed at the base. More about that story later.

There were three parties shortly after we arrived: Christmas, a Hail and Farewell, and a New Year's Eve party. The Air Force was great about welcoming new comers. We moved almost every three years, so we learned to make friends quickly. I still have some friendships that stretch all the way back to pilot training in 1975.

House Hunting

The realtor had one builder she worked for almost exclusively. He built a very nice, upscale house. We looked at about two dozen homes. None were perfect, but all were more than acceptable. As we were driving around one day, I saw a "For Sale by Owner" sign. The outside of the house caught my eye. I thought, "Leave it to Beaver."

Note: Leave It to Beaver was an American television situation comedy about an inquisitive and often times naive boy named Theodore "The Beaver" Cleaver and his adventures at home, in school, and around his suburban neighborhood. His parents were June and Ward Cleaver, and his brother was Wally. The show attained an iconic status in the US, with the Cleavers exemplifying the idealized suburban family of the mid-20th century.

I wanted the house to fulfill another of my dreams. I had grown up wishing I was "The Beaver," and my parents were June and Ward Cleaver. I did not have a "Leave it to Beaver" childhood, but my children would. What I was robbed of, they received. This was another reason I wanted to grow up with my children.

The location was close to the base, and about half of the residents were civilian and the other half, military – a good mix, really.

We met with the people next door who were helping the owners sell. The home owner, a Colonel, had moved from the North American Aerospace Defense Command (NORAD), Cheyenne Mountain, in Colorado Springs. He had the house built for him with lots of nice options: full brick around the first level and ceramic title in the entry way in place of wood. Neighbors who had gotten the wood option were disappointed, because it looked terrible in six months. The house had lots of upgrades. The Colonel and his family had lived in the house for only six months. Then, the Colonel got fired from his positon on base. He called NORAD and asked if he could get his old job back. They said they would be happy to have him. The Colonel and his family moved back to Colorado. That left their house vacant. I made an offer, and we had a new house. I delayed the closing date until the 15th of January, still concerned the Air Force might cancel my assignment. I told the realtor that I had purchased a home "For Sale by Owner," and she seemed a tad miffed. I had just cheated her out of a commission. Oh, well. Or was it?

I went out to the base to find my new squadron building and to introduce myself to the Commander. This time, I had a nice tight haircut, my shoes were shiny, and my uniform was squared away. He told me what the paperwork had told me – I wouldn't be theirs until after training. Still, I thought it a good idea to go by, say "Hello," and "Thank you!"

LBG Two

My wife and I were a watching a football game. It was approaching half-time, and she disappeared into the bathroom. She emerged and said, "I'm having contractions." I asked, "How far apart?" She responded, "Every three minutes." I thought, *Okay, here we go again.*

My wife had caught a stomach flu on the 26th of December. My son soon thereafter determined the life support system was going south on him. So, he decided to make a break for it, while he still could. When my daughter was born, I was like Donald Duck. This time, I was watching the football game, and it was only two minutes to half time. I asked her if she thought she could wait. Humor. She disappeared into the bathroom, got her "go bag", and then we were on our way to the base hospital. The doctor checked her out and said she was only three centimeters dilated. Two resident doctors were on duty, and they didn't want to call the boss. So, Mutt and Jeff dinked around for a while. They were going to send her back home. Then, one of the nurses said, "Let's wait thirty more minutes and check you again." In thirty minutes, they checked, and she was ten centimeters dilated. She was having a baby. The nurse said, "Do you feel like pushing?" My wife said, "Yes." The nurse got into her face and said, "Don't push." They asked me to put on some scrubs so I could be in the delivery room. I went next door and got dressed. When I returned a minute or two later, she was gone. I asked where she was. The nurse said, "They're in the delivery room. Hurry!"

Unlike her first pregnancy when she spent twenty hours in labor, this event was much faster. The doctor asked her to push. She did, but nothing happened. He asked her to push again, and we had a brand new baby boy. They let me cut the cord. Our son was born two days after Christmas in the year 1987. Our son opened his eyes and closed them right back up. We would find out later that he doesn't like change. We had another LBG: a Little Baby Guy.

My mother in-law, Ruth, came out the next day to help. There we were, one big, happy, little family: my wife, her mother, my daughter, my son and me, all together in a two-bedroom apartment. Cozy. In less than three weeks, we moved into our new home with considerably more room.

A Love Affair

The first day of class, there were only two student pilots. A brand newbie, right out of pilot training, and me. The instructor said, "Your orders are wrong. They say you're going to incur a two-year active duty service commitment. Actually, it's really three years. If anyone does not want to incur that commitment, raise your hand now and leave the room." The newbie had just graduated from pilot training and already had an eleven-year commitment. So, the instructor was talking to me. I took my left hand and put it under the left cheek of my ass followed by my right hand under the right cheek. I did it so the instructor could plainly see what I doing. He said, "Okay, then. At the completion of the course, you will have a three-year active duty service commitment."

What he didn't know about was my prior Marine Corps service. Because of it, I only had about three years and seven months to go to retirement. The Air Force normally won't reassign you if you have less than a year. They could have sent me someplace remote, without my family, for six months, but the odds were in my favor that they would not.

I entered C-9 training on January 4, 1988. It followed what was now a familiar pattern: ground school for a couple of weeks, with a comprehensive test at the end, followed by time spent in the simulator. The simulator time was contracted to Flight Safety in Saint Louis, by the airport. They did an excellent job. I was gone for a couple of weeks for that, leaving my wife at home with a newborn and our daughter. She had her hands full, and so did I.

I found flying the C-9 simulator easier than the C-130 simulator. We completed the course successfully, and I was on my way to our new home. The 912 didn't have a good heater in it. It was winter, and I was having trouble seeing where I was going. I got off at the wrong exit and was driving through a very bad part of town in the middle of the night. I thought, *great all this, and I'm going to get killed in East Saint Louis.* I didn't.

We had a couple of days off, and then we hit the flight line. There were three of us in the C-9: my classmate, the instructor and me. The instructor was in the right seat, I was in the left, and the other pilot was watching from the jump seat. You can learn a lot from the jump seat. Then, the co-pilot and I swapped seats, and it was his turn.

I had watched the video "High Flight" so many times growing up. I got to fly a couple of fighter type aircraft, the T-37 and T-38. It was cramped inside the cockpit, and I had to wear an oxygen mask and parachute. It wasn't quite what I thought it would be. I flew the C-130 for nine years and had about thirty-two hundred hours of flight time. It was fun, but it was really loud, vibrated and shook a lot. Because we were always playing in the mud, the aircraft was dirty, so the C-130 wasn't the dream either. I was still chasing my ultimate dream.

It was cold the first morning we flew, about 38-40 degrees, and we didn't need to de-ice the plane. The sky was a beautiful Southern Illinois Winter blue. There was no wind at all. We taxied out to the runway, lined up, and pushed the power to the takeoff setting. Soon, we began rolling down the runway. The engines on the C-9 are on the tail, and it was quiet inside the cockpit. The engines were loving the cold air. We lifted off. All those dreams from childhood came true that day and at that moment. It was everything I thought flying would be and then so much more. I fell in love – really, in love – with that aircraft. It was silky smooth with the controls feather light to the touch and no artificial hydraulic assist. We climbed effortlessly into the sky, and I was living "High Flight." It wasn't a fighter or a cargo airplane. It was civilized, and there I was.

We flew out and did some of the required maneuvers. Then, we returned to do some practice landings. When it came to landing, the C-9 was known as the "Great Humbler." You could set everything up correctly, and it would land beautifully smooth. We would call those landings a "Lubber." It was like someone had put grease on the runway, and you just slid it on. Other times, it was not so much smooth. You could set up the airplane the exact same way, with the same sight picture and the same power setting, and it would go, thump, ergo, the name the "Great Humbler."

My first landing was neither a "Lubber" nor a "Thump!" During my second landing, I was humbled. We stayed in the pattern and did multiple touch-and-goes. A touch-and-go is where the aircraft lands but doesn't stop. Instead, you keep rolling and do a takeoff. We would come around for more landings, go-arounds, and simulated engine-out procedures. It was all the air work required to learn how to fly the C-9.

I thought flying couldn't get any better than that first day. I was wrong. Oh, so terribly wrong. It was like each day was additive to the love from the day before. The C-9 had now become an "affair in my hands and in my heart."

In the Herk, you flew with combat boots, and it felt like it. I learned how to fly the C-9. We flew in combat boots, but it felt like flying with sneakers on. In a short time, it felt like I had on warm slippers, sitting beside a warm fireplace in the safety of my home with the lights turned down low and snow quietly falling outside. It was comfortable, to say the least. One day, something happened. I got into the cockpit, but it no longer felt like I was a foreign object occupying a space in her. I had become one with her – a connected part – a second skin, if you will.

"I pick the prettiest part of the sky, and I melt into the wing and then into the air, 'til I'm just a soul on a sunbeam." ~ Richard Bach

Words cannot adequately describe the feeling. Suffice it to say, I was living the dream – a love affair in full bloom. My wife was jealous. She said, "If it were another woman, I could compete. But how do I compete with an 110,000 pound piece of aluminum, rubber and glass?" Darlin', you can't.

In six months' time, I upgraded to captain and two months later to instructor. If you will remember, it took me four years to upgrade to instructor in C-130's. It was now obvious to everyone that not only could I fly, but I brought a spirit with me. The mission of the C-9 was aeromedical evacuation. The Nightingale, as she was called, was named after Florence Nightingale, a celebrated English social reformer, statistician and the founder of modern nursing. She came to prominence while serving as a nurse during the Crimean War, where she tended to wounded soldiers. She was a hero.

Although a lot of people thought the C-9 was a hospital in the sky, she was really an air ambulance. The crew consisted of eight people: two pilots (officers), two nurses (officers), three medical technicians (enlisted) and one enlisted mechanic. Most were handpicked and all top notch.

Of course, the pilots flew the plane. We normally had eight stops in one day. The average leg (flight) time was about fifty minutes. We would get into a rhythm – such a sweet rhythm. The adrenaline would pump through our veins.

We would literally hit the ground running as we left the plane. The cargo door would open, and a ramp would come down. The captain would go into base operations, get the weather report, and check the notice to airmen about possible issues at the next station. The captain would call back to base, but only if there was problem. The co-pilot would set up the cockpit for the next leg and get the ATIS. Even though the captain had gone inside for the weather, we still had to get the information and give ATC the identifier. As the captain was running back to the plane, the ramp would be coming up, and the cargo door would be closing. We would hop into our seats, call for our clearance, run checklists in record time, taxi out and be gone. The average ground time was ten to twenty minutes.

> *Note: Automatic Terminal Information Service, or ATIS, is a continuous broadcast of recorded non-control aeronautical information in busier terminal (i.e. airport) areas. ATIS broadcasts contain essential information, such as weather information, which runways are active, available approaches, and any other information required by the pilots, such as important NOTAMs. Pilots usually listen to an available ATIS broadcast before contacting the local control unit in order to reduce the controllers' workload and relieve frequency congestion.*

The recording is updated in fixed intervals or when there is a significant change in the information, e.g. a change in the active runway. It is given a letter designation (e.g. Bravo) from the ICAO spelling alphabet. The letter progresses through the alphabet with every update and starts at "Alpha" after a break in service of twelve hours or more. When contacting the local control unit, a pilot will indicate whether he or she has "information <letter>", where <letter> is the ATIS identification letter of the ATIS transmission the pilot received. This allows the ATC controller to verify whether the pilot has all the current information.

The nurses, like Florence Nightingale, were my heroes – angels in the sky. I learned to respect them a great deal and learned a new language. I called it "Medical-eze." They had both inflight and ground duties. They hustled the sick patients or passengers on and off the plane, did their medical charting and all the other stuff they did back there. There were rumors that the pilots worked for the nurses. Only a couple of times did that issue come up. I will go into greater detail about that later, but the pilot's job was to safely fly the plane and the nurse's was to care for the sick and wounded. The medical technicians worked for the nurses. They would carry litters and throw bags in the underside cargo holds. They also helped the nurses a lot with medical issues in the back.

The mechanic had no inflight duties. Their job was to maintain the aircraft on the ground. They put fuel and oil in the aircraft and repaired any malfunctions. We would let them sit in the jump seat and make radio calls to Operations with our estimated time of arrival and status and let them get the ATIS report for our destination. It made them feel good talking on the radios, and it didn't hurt us any. It was a really good job for the mechanic. Flight mechanics at home station would have to work for hours on end, but the inflight mechanic's mission as a crew member was fairly simple. He received flight pay and got to play with us.

After a long day, we would get to our hotel rooms and meet in the lobby to go out to dinner. There were normally five or six crew members there. Most times not everybody would come, but if only two or three showed up, it meant there had been an unresolved issue that day. Feelings sometimes got hurt.

Most of our trips lasted two and three days. We would return exhausted but energized at the same time. What most of the pilots really wanted to do was go fly again, myself included.

Additional duty

Shortly after I arrived at the squadron, I was assigned to be the Chief Scheduler. After all, I had all that scheduling experience in Alaska and Arkansas, but now I was the "Chief" in charge of the whole office.

The commander called me in to give me the assignment and a briefing. We got along very well. He gave me the assignment and then said, "We have a morale problem here, and I want you to find the cause and fix it." No one ever wants to be the *Morale Officer*. Most times, you weren't successful.

The scheduling office had a staff of seven, including myself. I got all my schedulers together and talked with them – not down to them. At first, they saw me as a major who was coming to make his "Spurs," which meant making a name for myself while screwing them over in the process. I was not about that at all. I just wanted to work with them. I told them the truth about how happy I was to be there flying the C-9 and how truly happy I was to be the new scheduling chief. Also, if they wanted to, they could scuttle me and get me fired. I told them I was pretty easy to work *with*, not for. I meant it all, and they sort of believed me. I had learned a lot in my Master's Program, Managerial Psychology, and now I would be given a chance to use some of it. I was team building.

As we set about doing our jobs, it didn't take long for them to figure out that I was telling them the truth. The previous Chief Scheduler had run the shop like a dictator, "Here's what you're going to do and when you're going to do it." I knew that was part of the morale problem. So, I ran the shop more like Monty Hall and "Let's Make a Deal." If a pilot wanted to change his or her schedule, I would hand them the scheduling book and say, "Here's the scheduling book. Find someone."

The scheduling book had all the assignments – who was flying and who was not. We had fifty-five pilots total, but only about forty were available to fly on a routine basis. The others were working at the Wing Headquarters and were seldom available to fly. They would only come out to keep themselves current in the airplane. They were required to have three take-offs and landings once every ninety days. Often times, they would get on and off the plane during an engine running on/off-load (ERO). During an ERO, you would open the door and get people on or off with the engines still running.

Sometimes, there was someone very easily available to fly. Other times, you had to get creative. At that point, I would help. When we found a possible solution, I would have the pilot call the scheduled pilot and ask if they would to be willing to change. If they were willing, I would get on the phone and give him or her the assignment. It was a good way to run the shop, and morale started to improve. The pilots, the schedulers and the powers-that-be saw the change.

One day, a pilot named Mike came running into the office. He said, "Todd." By then, in most informal situations they did not call me Major anymore. I liked that. "You have to get me off of my flight tomorrow. It's my wife's anniversary, and I forgot all about it." I asked, "Oh your wife's anniversary, but not yours?" He was completely frazzled. He said, "Oh yeah, mine too. Oh! You know what I mean." I did know but had to laugh. I gave him the book and said, "Find someone." He looked, and there was not an easy fix. Then, I jumped in and helped. We would have to move two pilots and change both of their assignments. You have to understand, we were scheduling with paper and pencils in those days. Schedulers normally had their hair on fire. It was one of the reasons schedulers didn't want to change assignments. It meant a lot of extra work for them, because any changes always had a ripple effect. The first change was easy. A two-day trip with an overnight in San Antonio. As a scheduler, it was important to know a little about your pilot's personal life. If they were having trouble at home, with the kids or whatever. Not enough to be nosey, but we had to pay attention.

Joe Bob was a character. I liked him a lot. He was easy-going all the time, always with a smile on his face and very happy-go-lucky. I knew Joe Bob had a female friend in San Antonio. That is why he requested San Antonio overnights all the time. Mike called him and asked if Joe Bob would make the trade. The answer was, "Oh, hell yes." The second trade was not as easy, but we worked it out. Mike told everyone about the "anniversary" event. After that, my stock value had gone up even further.

Still, my job of improving morale in the squadron was not finished. I had to assess all of my schedulers. In particular, one stood out. She was an Air Force Academy graduate. She would not work with the pilots. She would change pilots' schedules to get herself a good deal. A big scheduling, No-No. She wanted the training mission to do an engine running on/off-load outside the squadron building to pick her up. "To make me feel special," she said. In short, she was a major pain in the ass. I went to the Commander and reminded him of my charge to identify the problem for the low morale and fix it. I told him, "I have identified the problem, and I want her gone. I would rather go undermanned in the scheduling office than have her working for me." I explained what she was doing. All the while the Commander was sucking wind, as if saying, "Oh crap. Say it isn't so."

I found out shortly thereafter that while she worked for me, I didn't write her evaluation. Although I should have, the Commander did. The same commander I had just blown the whistle to. What? I had never heard of such a thing. If I didn't write her evaluation, I didn't have any real control over her. It seems that some general at the academy was impressed with her, and she was going to make general, come hell or high water. The Commander was under orders to make sure that her career progressed accordingly. About three weeks later, she was reassigned to the Administration Office. I went undermanned in the shop and didn't regret it at all.

When I first arrived at the squadron, the halls were quiet. In six months' time there was a lot of noise – the sweet sound of laughter. The Scheduling Office became the place to be and hang out. I brought a popcorn popper in from home, and most times, there was the sweet smell of warm popcorn in the hall. We always had hot coffee and hot chocolate available. The morale of the squadron had improved.

I always answered the phone in my Scheduling Office in the following manner, "11th AAS, MAC's finest, Major Howe." This left the person on the other end of the phone wondering if the 11th AAS was MAC's finest or me. The answer to that question was, "Yes." A number of people took notice of it, and the squadron received MAC's Best Airlift Squadron of the Year Award. In receiving the award, the Commander made reference to my contribution for that accomplishment. *Well, hell yeah.*

The Hughes Program

A couple of months later, Lt. Col. Hughes from MAC headquarters, only a couple blocks away, came to our squadron. He had written a computer program to help with scheduling. He said our squadron was perfect for a Beta test – whatever that was. Our squadron was small and any kinks could be worked out here first. I told him I didn't know a thing about computers. He said, "Perfect. The program is designed for people just like you." He talked me into it. He provided all the equipment and showed me how to input the data. After a short, ninety-minute tutorial, we started the Beta test.

It didn't have a mouse at first and really needed one. We would have to select a pilot's name and move it by the left, right, up and down keys on the keyboard. Someone was looking over my shoulder and said, "You need a mouse." I didn't even know what a mouse was, but I called Lt. Col. Hughes, and asked him for one. A few days later, he showed up with a computer disk, upgraded the program and gave me a mouse. The program worked incredibly well. Where the schedulers used to be running about like their hair was on fire, they now sat with very little to do. Someone would come by with a change request and a few key strokes later the problem was solved.

Scheduling was a lot more than just moving one body from one place to another. The FAA and Air Force had rules about how many hours you can fly in day, a week, a month and how much crew rest you needed before or after a flight. All of the requirements and potential pitfalls were addressed in the program. If the scheduler tried to do something wrong, the program would tell them about it in big red letters.

Then, a self-proclaimed computer expert told us we needed to tie the entire wing into a *network*. His program was a freaking disaster. You couldn't get on the network to input data, and it crashed a few times every day. His network program was *trash*. We got a new Operations Officer, and I told him about the two competing programs. I told him ours worked, the other did not, and we should continue to use the Hughes program. He listened, then came to me the next day and said the computer expert had sold him on the idea of the network. So much for my salesmanship. That day, I deactivated the Hughes program and went on the network. None of the orders for the flights were done. Nothing was getting accomplished. After about three days of this chaos, the Operations Officer came in and said, "Let's run both programs simultaneously until the bugs are worked out of the network." When I left two years later, the network still didn't work.

The First Two Years

The first two years of flying and scheduling were fantastic. The Commander wanted to help get me promoted and moved me to be the Officer-in-Charge of Administration. The same woman that I had fired early was there. She was working for me again, and I still didn't write her evaluation. I did that job for about eight months. I was then reassigned to Instructor Flight. There were just two of us in the office. The other pilot was senior to me, but he ran the shop like we were both in charge. I was continuing to fly.

After two years, we got a new Squadron Commander. A man named Lt. Col. Rick. His wife was the realtor we screwed out of her commission when buying our house. *Oh, boy!* I can't make this stuff up.

Just a Few "There I Was" Flights

There I was…flying a mission into Louisville, Kentucky. The weather – always the weather – was terrible. We had thunder storms in all quadrants. Approach control kept giving us different runways to land on because the winds were changing so rapidly. This flight was not as bad as the one in Alaska with the Herk, but it was close. Finally, they assigned a runway that would work. As we were on final approach, the wind was howling and gusting at plus or minus thirty knots. The copilot started yelling out, "You're below the glide path." We had just lost about two-hundred feet in altitude, but we were still six-hundred feet above the ground. I remember my calm demeanor. It was as surprising to me then as it is now. I said, "Yes, but look at the airspeed and throttle position." The airspeed was reading thirty knots *slow* and the throttles were at full maximum. A short time later, we were fast and back on glide path, then above the glide path and fast. I didn't pull the power back. When we landed, we were on glide slope on airspeed and on center line. It was one of my best "Lubbers" ever. There must have been two or three inches of water on the runway. Nice and smooth.

Shortly before our flight happened in Louisville, a Delta Flight, landing at the Dallas Fort Worth airport had similar conditions. They chased the glide slope and pulled the power back when the airspeed showed they were going too fast. Then, they ran out of airspeed, stalled, and everyone on board was killed. I learned a lot from other's mistakes. By the way, I flew the same profile, as the Delta crash, in the simulator and survived.

There I was…we were on an emergency air evacuation mission. The weather was horrendous. We were at 33,000 feet and had the weather radar inside the aircraft turned on. We saw hooks, which are tornados. Even if you're above them, you need to avoid them. They do nasty things to airplanes. It was kind of like what you see in the movies. Lightning was flashing, there was Saint Elmo's fire all around us, and again, we had a handful of airplane. It was at that time that the charge flight nurse came into the cockpit and told me we had to land. She was attempting to fly my airplane from the doorway. I told her, "This is not a good time." She continued getting more forceful in her voice. I said, "Alita get out of here. I'm flying the airplane, not you, and I'm trying to keep us alive. Co-pilot, close the door." He slammed the door in her face. Like I said earlier, most of the nurses were first rate, but some tried to run the show.

There I was... flying into Kelly Air Force Base in San Antonio. I should have had Joe Bob with me. The weather was scary ugly, with colors I had never seen before or since. Then Approach called us and said, "There are Level Six thunder storms in all quadrants." I asked, "I thought the rating scale only went up to level five?" He said, "It does, but this is level six." Comforting.

There I was...on a training mission with two other pilots and a mechanic. We were in Colorado, practicing high altitude approaches, missed approaches and engine-out work. We were on our way back to Scott when we stopped in Colorado Springs to get some fuel. Operations called with a request. They had an enlisted man whose father had suffered a heart attack. The enlisted man was on emergency leave. His father was located in New Athens, Illinois. We were going to Scott which was close, so I said, "We can take him." On route, I went back and talked with the young man. He was in a state. You could tell he was very concerned about his dad. I asked him what his plans were to get to New Athens. He didn't have any. He was going to go to Scott and try to work something out from there. I went back to the flight deck and checked our manuals. First, I needed to find out if New Athens had an airport. If so, could we land there legally? The manuals indicated we could. I went back and talked with the young man again. I asked him if it would help if we dropped him off in New Athens. He asked, "Can you do that?" After all, that would put him right in his home town. I told him we could. I went back to the flight deck, called Air Traffic Control and asked to change our flight plan to New Athens. ATC said they could but asked if there was problem. I explained everything to ATC, and he asked, "Can you do that?" It saved the young man a lot of travel time, depending on his transportation availability. It was a good day to be a C-9 pilot.

One other story needs to be mentioned. We were flying on the East Coast from Andrews AFB in Maryland to Pope AFB, North Carolina. We were supposed to continue through the Southeast U.S. to Biloxi, Mississippi and then home to Scott. When we landed at Pope, I went inside to Base Operations to have a look at the weather map. It was even uglier than I suspected. The weather forecaster suggested we get airborne as soon as possible. I said, "We're not going into that or anywhere near it." I walked across the hall and changed my flight plan back to Andrews. And from there, we went back home to Scott. I bring this up because one of the nurses came to me later and said she was concerned about our safety during that flight. I liked her very much and apologized to her. I had done everything by the book and safely, but I didn't like people on my airplane to ever be concerned about their safety. Perhaps, I should have told her about my covenant with God.

Promotion

I swear the Air Force must have been schizophrenic. They were always changing the evaluation and promotion systems. In March of 1990, I was in my promotion cycle for Lt. Col.

One day, the Commander, Rick, called me into his office. He was there and so was the Operations Officer, Major Mike-Mike. Mike had been my check airman at Little Rock when I upgraded to instructor in 1980. We had a bond. Rick asked me to close the door. *Gulp!* The three of us now sat in one room together. My mind was racing. *Oh no! If they found out about this or that I am so totally screwed.* The other three things I could talk my way out of easily enough.

They sat me down with the table between us. This was also not a good sign. Rick then asked me, "What is it going to take to keep you in the Air Force Todd?" Okay. So, this wasn't about an ass-chewing. This was going to be my promotion board. They knew about the short stick I had drawn at Hickam. Yes, it had soured me some, but my plan was still to retire in August of 1991. They knew my plans and were trying to get me to stay in.

I said, "It is going take two things." Rick asked, "Okay, what are they?" I said, "The first one is a promotion." Rick said, "That's what this is all about." *Like I didn't know that already?* The Commander could give me one of three recommendations: definitely promote, promote or don't promote. With the first option, I had a really good chance. With the second option, my chances were less likely. With the third option, I would have no chance of promotion at all. Then, Rick asked, "What is the other thing?" I told him, "A job." Rick asked, "What job do you want?" I looked at the two men sitting in front of me. I pointed to Mike and said, "First, I want your job, and then I pointed to Rick, and then I want yours." Rick thought a moment and said, "Todd, you're not on that career path." I already knew that, but Rick said he could get me a good job at the Wing where I would be able to continue to fly. They knew how much I loved the flying. I asked him which Wing jobs. Rick listed five – all of them were Lt. Col. Positions at the Wing. One of them actually sounded pretty good. It was called Current Operations and the office was co-located in our squadron building. Lt. Col. Don M, a good friend, had the job but was planning to leave. I said, "If that's all you have for me, then don't waste a promotion on me." Rick said, "It wouldn't be a wasted promotion." My feelings were still hurt from Hickam. Besides, I was planning to get out and work for the airlines. The airlines were still hiring.

I don't know what Rick's recommendation was, but I didn't get promoted. It stung a little bit, but I had bigger plans.

DC-9 Type Rating

The C-9 Squadron had made an arrangement with a reserve C-9 pilot, who also happened to be an FAA Check Airman. He could administer a civilian DC-9 Type Rating while, at the same time, issuing an ATP (Air Transport Pilot) rating. An ATP is the highest rating you can get flying airplanes. It's sort of like the PhD of flying. It was a big deal, since you needed one to get hired by the airlines.

First, there was a lot of home study for a written examination. There was a school that taught the test. I went to the school, studied at home for a couple of weeks, took the test and passed. All of this was paid for by me. Then, two applicants would fly from Scott AFB to Minneapolis, Minnesota where the C-9 check airman was. This would be accomplished on a local area training mission. Normally, these training missions don't leave home base.

The next phase of the type rating was an oral examination and a practice simulator ride. The next day, we had the simulator check ride. On Day Three, the local area trainer returned to take us home. Before we departed for Scott, we hopped on the C-9 with the Check Airman, and he administered the check rides. Each check ride lasted about ninety minutes. We covered most everything. Then, we returned to Minneapolis for lunch and a debriefing. My debriefing lasted less than five minutes. I passed and now had a DC-9 Type Rating, along with an ATP rating. The local trainer then took us home. This was considered by the Air Force as "temporary duty," and we received *extra* pay for it. The downside was…Nope, there was no downside.

My Last Year

It was the last year of the third trimester of my summer, and it was the best year of my life. I told you earlier that I was fortunate enough to have two "Summers of '42." The first was when I was seventeen. The second was when I turned forty-two in August of 1990. That same day, Iraq invaded Kuwait. The crew got together and had a birthday cake on the first leg of the flight that day. They lit some candles, and along with the passengers, wished me a happy birthday with song. Moments like those are what you'll remember for a lifetime.

We're going to War

How could going to war be a good thing? Lt. Col. Rick, trying to crush any and all rumors, called all of the pilots together in the secure briefing room. He locked the door and told us what we were going to do.

We were going to the United Arab Emirates and would fly air evacuation casualties from the Forward Operating Area back to the base in the Emirates. We would be replaced in the states with a C-130 reserve unit. Then, he asked, "Are there any questions? Yes, Major Howe." I asked, "Does anyone else in this room beside Mike and myself have any Combat Aircrew Training?" He answered, "No." So I asked, "Are we going to repaint our planes and remove the aiming stake on the tail?" Again, he answered, "No, because according to the Geneva Convention, the enemy can't shoot at ambulances – ours included. We would be identified by the cross on the tail of the C-9." There were no warm feelings there for me. I then asked, "Because we have status, we're not going to be allowed to take resupplies to the front lines, is that correct?" The answer was, "Yes. You are correct. We will be restricted from doing that." I said, "The C-9 is a civilian aircraft with a single wiring system. The C-130 has a triple wiring bundle – three times redundant. The C-130, not having ambulance status, can carry supplies to the Forward Operating Area. It can also take out the wounded. Plus, the crews are all Combat Aircrew Training qualified. Wouldn't it be a better idea to have the C-130 unit go to the Emirates and leave us here?"

I was the only one in the room that had been to war, and I was the only one in the room that didn't want to go. At worst you could get killed or wounded. But no matter what happened, we were going be uncomfortable. Rick said, "It doesn't matter. We going to war." There was a cheer from audience. I was silent. *Clueless children.*

About four days later, CINC MAC, the four star general in charge of it all, said, "Am I the only one around here who's thinking?" He then listed all the things I had brought up in the briefing room. Either someone in the room had talked to someone or the General knew his shit. I'm with the latter. We exchanged places with the C-130 unit, and we were now going to Myrtle Beach, South Carolina. A better option, I thought, than the Emirates. The commander never said a word to me about it. He did, however, call me in to his office before the deployment and said, "Todd, I know you're not doing anything wrong." Translation: *I think you are, but I can't prove it.* He went on and said, "The deployment site will be a target-rich environment for rumors, and I wouldn't want that to happen." Message heard and received. He was going to keep me under control. I was still the wild child.

Note: Like Mark Twain said before me, "The reports of my death have been greatly exaggerated." Likewise, the rumors of my exploits were also greatly exaggerated.

Deployment

On our flight into Myrtle Beach, Approach Control had gotten us in close and high. I asked for clearance for a visual approach. Approach Control was used to working with fighters and said, "You can't make it from there." I said, "I can't if you won't give us the clearance." The controller cleared me for the approach. The C-9 would drop out of the sky. The trick was to slow the airplane down and then dirty it up – putting down the gear and all the flaps. The maximum setting with fifty degree flaps had a limiting airspeed of one-hundred-and-eighty knots. I descended at between one-hundred-and-seventy-five to one-hundred-and-seventy-eight. We called the tower and asked for permission to land. They said, "Cleared to land, if you think you can make it from there." The next trick was to do a two-step approach. I had to fly the C-9 at high speed, go *below* the glide path and then pull the nose up. The airspeed would bleed off very quickly. I landed in the zone, on airspeed and on center line. *LUBBER.*

The Commander and some of his staff were there to greet us. Before deployment I had gone to a pet store and bought a dog leash – a chain with a leather handle. I got off the airplane with the dog chain around my neck. I walked over to the Commander and saluted smartly. He asked, "What's with the dog chain?" I said, "Sir, you said you wanted to keep me on a short leash while we're here. So, I thought I would help out and bring the leash." You have admit that's funny. The Commander didn't see the humor in it at all. His jaws locked a little. I just gave him my normal shit-eatin' grin.

I tried throughout the deployment to get a female nurse or female pilot to put teeth marks in the leather handle. I didn't have any takers, but the squadron heard about the leash incident and got a picture of me on a bed with four or five females. Clothes on, of course.

The Air Force housed us at a place called the Sheridan Hotel. I had a fifteenth story room overlooking the Atlantic Ocean. Maids came in everyday to make my bed. I don't remember this happening when I was in Vietnam.

When we arrived at the deployment base, we had already won the war. Let the parties begin! *Oh my, and didn't they!* The deployment only lasted five days. I'm glad it didn't last a week. I don't drink, but I don't think I could have survived. When we returned to Scott, I was in the back of the plane and slept the whole flight.

My last air evac mission

Getting Short

My second 'Summer of 42' was in midseason now. I was passed over a second time for promotion. At the end of the Gulf War, they started downsizing the military. I was to retire on August 1st 1991. On October 1st 1991, they would have forced me out of the service without a pension, healthcare and all the other benefits that come with a retirement. Do you still doubt that I have a Guardian Angel? Well, don't!

Just like in Vietnam, I was getting "short" now. I was going to retire and fly for the airlines. *Or was I?* After the war, commercial airline hiring slowed and then almost stopped completely. Unlike the Marines where I did not look back, here I did. I had left the best flying assignment of my career behind. I had left the best of it all behind. It broke my heart. My heart is broken still.

My fini-flight

The Road Not Taken.
Robert Frost.
Two roads diverged in a yellow wood,
And sorry I could not travel both
And be one traveler, long I stood
And looked down one as far as I could
To where it bent in the undergrowth;

Then took the other, as just as fair,
And having perhaps the better claim
Because it was grassy and wanted wear,
Though as for that the passing there
Had worn them really about the same,

And both that morning equally lay
In leaves no step had trodden black.
Oh, I kept the first for another day!
Yet knowing how way leads on to way
I doubted if I should ever come back.

I shall be telling this with a sigh
Somewhere ages and ages hence:
Two roads diverged in a wood, and I,
I took the one less traveled by,
And that has made all the difference

I can appreciate the poetic value and symbolic beauty of the poem, "The Road Not Taken" by Robert Frost, but from a pragmatic perspective, how could he possibly know? He did not travel both roads. So, he could not know which of the two made the greater difference. Either road he took was either the correct or the wrong one. Therein lies the dilemma. He will or at least should forever wonder if he chose the right one.

The missing chapter

It will be my next book

Fall

In Fall the river runs quieter now, deeper and wider the waters. It is as if the river has finally found its purpose. It is content to remain within the banks. Continuing on with its journey.

Ecstasy and Agony: A Love Affair Ended

I retired on August 1, 1991. I was forty-two. Two days later, I turned forty-three. Summer had morphed into fall — right at its scheduled arrival time. Another 21-year season had come and passed.

A Love Gone Forever

"Don't play in the street," they said. "You could get hurt," they said. But I was young and foolish. One day I walked over to the curb and touched it with my toe. It did not hurt me. Another day passed, and I put one foot on the street and then the other. It still did not hurt me — did not hurt me at all. "They were wrong," I said, and I went running into the street, my hands and arms waving in the air, reaching out for the sky and squealing with a delight. I had never experienced this before, you see — this running in the street. I was completely and utterly free. My euphoria, you see — running in the street that day.

So, I did not hear nor see it coming, but come it did. And there was a great crash followed by a deep falling. There must have been horns, lights or warnings of some sort. Perhaps, there were. Perhaps, I chose not to see nor hear them. For I was running in the street you see. I was free, and it didn't hurt me.

Then, I fell into a deep sleep for a very short while – three years seven months, I am told. While I was away, I dreamed. I was on soft clouds, floating weightlessly – flying without my plane with no worries or concerns.

It was actually most wonderful there. A beautiful angel took care of me. She was better to me than I deserved, you see, for I had played in the street that day. She held my hand and then my heart, and I, in turn, held hers. As long as we held each other tight, we knew we would never return. I had run in the street that day, you see. My euphoria set me free, and it didn't hurt me or anyone else. My joy and my glee.

Then, I heard wee small voices crying out to me, and I started to awaken. I tried to ignore the voices. I tried so hard to stay asleep, but I couldn't. When I awoke, I let go of the angels hand while desperately trying to hold on. She took her hand and heart that day, never to return. I had gone to sleep a boy, you see, and had woken up a man. The pain was so intense at first and then because unbearable. You see, "You're not supposed to play in the street," they said, "You could get hurt," they said.

They said, "In time the wound would heal." Who knows? It may someday, but it still hurts when I remember the euphoria of running in the street that day and holding the angels hand so tight so that she would never go away. I try not to remember now the euphoria and the pain. But I do, you see, and I wouldn't have it any other way. Emotions are my memories now, and they are with me every day.

"Don't run in the street," they said. "You could get hurt," they said. I played in the street that day and got hurt so very badly.

The great question of all time. "Is It Better to Have Loved and Lost, Than to Never Have loved At All?"

Let me leave you with this:

Go play in the street today. You may not have a tomorrow.

My Difficult Time

I now, sort of, laugh at what I called my "difficult time." It was my transition from the Air Force to civilian life, but there is nothing really funny about severe depression nor an emotional breakdown. Knowing what it is, coupled with all the education I had and having made all the preparations does little good when the battle is between you and your mind. It happens when you think it cannot happen to you, because you "know." You're too smart, and you are above it all. Cock sure of myself, I was. I thought myself too strong, too smart and found I was not. So many things happened at once: loss of identity, friends and purpose. I worried about caring for those I had pledged to care for, about my income being cut by two-thirds, and the list goes on. But I knew what the real problem was: the thought that I might never fly again. Flying to me was a love *that* deep and strong.

I woke up one morning, and I was sitting on my pity pot, totally stressed out and worrying about everything. Then, for one brief moment, I thought, "Maybe it would be better if I wasn't here." Immediately thereafter, I thought, "Well, that's crazy. How could my not being here solve any of my problems?" I had hit rock bottom.

You are never the same after an event like that – nor was I. I still had my happy-go-lucky, give-a-shit exterior. That was my facade – my safety and protection. But deep inside, I was changed. I was now more guarded than I was before. Many people seem to like the new me. I don't as much. People who knew me before now say I am more caring, sincere and decent. I don't know. I'll let them decide. I am enough of a narcissist not to care what others think about me.

"When you are truly comfortable with who you are, not everybody will like you. But you won't care about it one bit." Unknown

After my breakdown, I started to rebuild. I enrolled in a Boeing 737 Type Rating class. It was very stressful. I needed the rating so I could apply to Southwest Airlines, where my friend Mac worked. There was a of lot home study, which I devoted myself to completely. Then, I had to go to Denver for ground school and simulators. I already had a type rating in the DC-9 and an ATP, so I could get my type rating in the simulator only. I wouldn't have to pay to ride in the airplane, which saved me a lot of money.

I was also interviewing during this time. I was turned down by Delta and American due to hearing loss. At UPS, I just failed the interview. Actually, it was a good thing in the long run.

Job Interview

While I was going through the Type Rating School in Denver, I interviewed with Alaska Airlines. It was in November 1991. I was still in deep depression recovery. I flew from Denver to Seattle. Alaska had arranged a hotel room for me. The next day at 5 am, I was scheduled for a simulator check ride. I walked into the briefing room and met my evaluator. He wanted to know if I was going to fly for the Air Force Reserve while working for Alaska. I told him no – I wasn't eligible to do that. He got a puzzled look on his face and asked, "Why not?" I said, "I retired from the military." He quickly grabbed my folder and looked up my age. I looked much younger than I was. I found out later that Alaska staff didn't have a high opinion of retired military pilots. This, because of jobs like in the C-9 Wing where pilots would only come out to fly once every ninety days. We talked, and he told me I would be the first to be evaluated in the simulator.

My partner was a check airman from another airline who was also interviewing at Alaska because he thought his company was going out of business. Our evaluator was a B-727 pilot and claimed not to know the MD-80 all that well. We went into the MD-80 simulator, and he asked, "Where is the antiskid switch on this aircraft?" I was looking forward and said, "On the C-9, it is right here," as I reached back and touched the switch without looking. Okay, I knew the aircraft. The co-pilot, my simulator partner, was having trouble setting the rudder pedals. On Boeing aircraft, there was a handle that you cranked either to the left or right to get the rudder pedals closer or further away from you. On the MD-80/DC-9, there was a knob. As a pilot, you would pull the knob towards you, kick the pedals to free them, then set the pedals where you wanted them, and release the knob. I instructed my partner on how to do it.

The evaluator set the simulator aircraft on center line, and we started rolling. At first, the aircraft veered slightly to the right, and I thought, "I can do better than this." I put the aircraft dead center on the runway. We took off without any issues. The first maneuver the evaluator wanted me to do was to enter a holding pattern. There are rules on entering a holding pattern. He set it up so I only had a three-degree difference between turning left or right for the entry hold. I turned in the correct direction. Then, I started the approach. I had everything set up for my outbound leg, and then the evaluator added a strong crosswind component, attempting to get me off course. I had to make a large correction but did so successfully. During the entire approach, I continually checked my instrument readings with my simulator partner by calling out what I saw. We arrived at our missed approach point, didn't see the runway and executed a missed approach.

The next maneuver was a precision approach with a course center line and a glide slope. Again, he brought me within a few degrees of a left or right turn. I turned in the correct direction again. He then put the simulator on "Hold," stopped it completely. This is seldom a good sign in the simulator. He asked, "Which way are you going to turn next?" I told him, "It will be a left-hand turn to intercept the inbound course inbound or to proceed direct to the beacon, followed by a right-hand turn outbound after crossing over the beacon for the approach." He said, "Well, there's no sense wasting any more time here. You obviously know what you're doing." All I heard was, "No sense wasting any more time here."

He then took control of the simulator and repositioned the aircraft for the precision approach. He asked, "Are you ready?" I said, "Yes." He then released the simulator and my course needle went from one side of my instrument panel to the center. I had to immediately roll into about forty degrees of bank to capture the center line. As soon as I did that, the glideslope came down fast from the top of the case, and I had to force the aircraft nose down about fifteen degrees to capture the glideslope. These abrupt maneuvers are not normally used. We were then supposed to proceed to the decision height, see the runway and land. When we got to the decision height, instead of seeing the runway, like he had told us initially we would, we saw nothing. So, I executed another missed approach. He made some lame excuse about putting the wrong runway in the simulator profile. Sure he did. Then, it was my simulator partner's turn. It was easy for him. There were no "Setups."

We had to take a psychological test, the Minnesota Multiphasic Personality Inventory (MMPI).

Note: "The MMPI is the most widely used and researched standardized psychometric test of adult personality and psychopathology. Psychologists and other mental health professionals use various versions of the MMPI to develop treatment plans; assist with differential diagnosis; help answer legal questions forensic psychology; **screen job candidates during the personnel selection process;** *or as part of a therapeutic assessment procedure."*

After the test, my partner and I went out to lunch and he asked, "What was that all about?" He was referring to my check ride. After all, he was a check airman at his airline. He said, "The evaluator tried to set you up four or five times to fail." I said, "Yeah, I know. They don't think retired military pilots can fly. I just proved them wrong."

That afternoon, I had my interview board. There was a MD-80 check airman, Capt. Cookem, a B-737 check airman, a woman from Human Resources Development and my simulator check airman. I had to dig down deep into my reserves. I had to give it everything I had. The evaluator asked me how I thought I had done on the check ride. I said, "I think I did okay, but I fly the aircraft better." He said, "Well, I think you did great." They then peppered me with questions for the next forty-five minutes. I was digging deeper and deeper into that reserve. Finally, it was over.

They asked me to wait outside in the lobby. I waited for what seemed like a lifetime. Finally, a woman from administration, Betsy (same name as my wife), came out with a big smile on her face and said Alaska would like me to stay another day and get a physical examination.

I had dinner with a couple of C-9 friends that now flew for Alaska. I told them I didn't know if I had a job or not. They both laughed and said the company wouldn't have asked me to stay if they weren't going to hire me. *Whew!*

The next day, I took my physical. I had a little trouble at first with the eye examination, but then I read the entire line. There was no depth perception test. Then, the nurse/technician administered the hearing test. I asked her, "Is this the type of test that if I don't pass you won't tell me?" She said, "No Todd. This is the type of test that if you don't pass it the first time I'll give you a second and third chance." I had trouble with the high frequency hearing levels. At the completion of the test, the technician said, "I see you have some high frequency loss of hearing, but that's okay. Alaska Airlines only cares about the conversational levels, and you passed those and the test."

I then talked with a doctor. He asked when my class start date was. I told him I didn't know if I even had a job yet. He just smiled. It seemed Alaska Airlines, being pennywise, wouldn't pay for the physical unless there was a job offer.

I had dug down deeper and harder than any other time in my life. I passed the simulator check, the interviews and the physical. I did all this while I was still suffering from major depression disorder. Damn, dreams don't come easy.

I Was Hired. Or Was I?

The class start date was scheduled to begin on January 2, 1992. While I was in Denver, I received a phone call from Alaska Airlines. This was right after my B-737 Type Ride check in the simulator, which I passed. I now had a DC-9 and a B-737 Type Rating. In fact, I received the phone call while we were debriefing the simulator check ride. Alaska offered me a Flight Officer's position. I received that news at about 10 am and was, of course, on top of the world. I got another call from Alaska about forty-five minutes later. They said there was a problem with the thyroid values on my physical – the high being a little too high and the low being a little too low. My offer of employment was rescinded, pending me retaking the blood test. I went to a lab in Denver and had the thyroid test redone. I told them not to fax the results to Alaska Airlines unless the numbers were favorable. I was going to keep taking that test until I passed it. The numbers were good, and the lab faxed the results. I waited.

Alaska didn't let me know one way or the other. A friend of mine at Alaska told me I was hired. Still, I waited. On the seventh of December, Pearl Harbor Day, I received a phone call from a woman in Human Resources named Rita. She had been on my interview board. She said, "Todd, I'm sorry, but I am afraid I have some bad news for you." My first thought was, "Oh no, they're not going to hire me after all." Then, she said, "Your class date has been moved back to the March, April or perhaps even May time frame, but *please,* say you're still interested in Alaska Airlines." I thought, "Please?" Wow. I told her I was. It was where I wanted to be. I went on and explained, "I still haven't received any verification of employment." She said she would write a letter and get it to me. I never received that letter in the mail. On my first day of class, there it was in my folder.

I received a phone call on Thursday, February 3, 1992. I was in my home in O'Fallon, Illinois, outside Saint Louis. It was a woman from Alaska Airlines personnel. She was cold and matter of fact. She said, "We are offering you a Flight Officer's position at Alaska Airlines beginning on the fourteenth of February." Yes, Valentine's Day. "The class begins at 8:30 am sharp in the Flight Operations Training Building. If you are here, your employment will begin at that date and time. If you are not here, the job offer is null and void, and don't ever apply to Alaska Airlines again!" *Wow!* I had a job. She said, "Alaska doesn't have a reciprocal agreement with an airline in Saint Louis."

Note: A reciprocal agreement allows pilots from one airline to fly on aircraft from other airlines – normally, in the jump seat.

She went on, "But, if you can get to Denver, we can get you a seat." I told her I wouldn't need the seat. I would drive out. She was quiet for a long moment and finally asked, "You can be here by the 14th? Driving?" I told her, "Even if the class were to begin, on Monday, in five days, I would be there."

Before Class

I drove to Portland a few days early. My father had developed advanced Alzheimer's disease. I was sitting in the living room with him, watching TV. He was in a fog. Then, out of nowhere he said, "So, you fly airplanes, do you?" I thought, "Oh-My-God, we're going to have a conversation." I said, "Yes, Dad. I do, and some say I'm pretty good at it." Then, he said, "Now let me get this straight. You were in the military for twenty years and got a pension with benefits right?" I said, "Yes, Dad. That's right." He then said, "And I worked at the post office for thirty-four years before I could get my pension." I replied, "Yes." Then, he said, "You are crooked, aren't you." He had a beautiful smile on his face, and he was so proud of me and my accomplishments. Still, he would never be able to just come out and say it. It was not who he was. We talked for a little while about where I was going. Then, all of a sudden, I noticed a strange look on his face. He didn't know who I was. He had slipped back into the fog. That was the last conversation I had with my father. The flame of anger, hatred, and bitterness I had harbored toward him had burned itself out years before. The embers were now arctic cold, but I didn't get a chance to tell him that I had forgiven him and that I loved him.

I got to Seattle a day early and had dinner with my two Alaska Airlines pilot friends, Don M. and Mark. Both were also C-9 pilots from Scott AFB. They told me they had heard a rumor that one half of the class would be going to the B-727 and the other half to the B-737/200. I said, "I have a type rating in the B-737. Should I ask for that?" They both simultaneously raised they hands in front of them and waved them from left to right saying, "*No!*" I asked, "What?"They said, "You don't want anything to do with the B-737 program here. It is bad news." They went on to explain to me in great detail the problems with the program. After our little talk, I said, "I'll take the B-727. I'm sure I'll be the oldest guy in the class, and they do it by seniority, right?"

My Holiday Year

In my first year, at Alaska, there were three major contract disputes between labor and management. Twice, the company put razor wire around the training center. I started working at Alaska Airlines on February 14, 1992. My father died on Thanksgiving Day that year. I received a furlough notice on Christmas Eve. I was to be furloughed on February 1, 1993, thirteen days before getting off probation. That meant the company had no obligation to recall me. My furlough was cancelled six-and-a-half hours before it was to take effect. I was numb to it all. This wasn't the dream I had hoped for.

One good thing about it was that I had requested and been awarded the 7th through the 21st of February off for vacation. When the furlough was cancelled, crew scheduling assigned me the first through the fifth of the month off. I called Craig, one of the "good" crew schedulers, and asked if he could trade a day off at the end of the month for the sixth. He said, "Todd, we're not supposed to do that, but the way they've been effing with you guys —Yes, I'll do it for you." I then had the 1st through the 21st of February off. I was supposed to have a check ride prior to the end of my probationary period. On the first of the month, I flew down to Phoenix and met with my friend Mac and his son, Mikey. We drove up to the Grand Canyon and went hiking.

Training scheduling called my wife and they wanted me to come off vacation to take a check ride. My wife told them I was at the Grand Canyon and that she couldn't get in touch with me. She told me this one evening when I was at a hotel in Flagstaff. There was *some* communication. Eff me. Eff them.

Let the Games Begin

But allow me to take you back to my first days at Alaska Airlines. I was in the training center building early and found the classroom. I got my bearings. At 8:30 am sharp, training started. First, the VP in charge of Operations and Chief Pilot (both the same person) came and welcomed us all to Alaska Airlines. He told us how great it was going to be. We would all be Captains in five years and make millions of dollars. My understanding is they give this same briefing to all the new hire classes at all the airlines.

We had to sign all kinds of paperwork. I was afraid I had signed away my firstborn male child. They talked with us about benefits. They mentioned the retirement plans. There was an A plan, defined benefit, and a B plan, a 401K. I didn't know which one to take, but someone else asked the question: *Which one do we take?* The presenter said, "You get both." That took up most of the morning. Then, they issued the aircraft assignments. According to the contract, it was supposed to be done by age seniority. It wasn't. Our union said we could file a grievance, but we were on probation for a year and if we did the company would fire us.

I, of course, was assigned to the B-737. The first two instructors apologized to us for putting new hires into the B-737 program. Two more warned us not to have an opinion – not to say anything to anyone unless asked – to keep our heads down and our mouths shut.

Then the B-737 Equipment Manager, Captain Stomper, came into the room. He was all huffy and pissed. He said the following, "I want you to know I didn't want new hires put into *my* program. You were forced on me. I like to pick and choose who it is that comes into *my* program, and I pick and choose who will be successful. I routinely washout one-third of those who attempt to upgrade in *my* program. So, you can look around at the six of you. Two of you will not be here on graduation day. Anyone who fails to successfully complete training will be terminated from Alaska Airlines." He then left the room the way he came in. I was stunned. *Really? What a throw-back!* All six of us made it through the program, despite Captain Stomper.

I completed the hardest training program in the airline industry at the time. It had a thirty-three percent failure rate. That figure, we would find out later, was greater than the FAA allows. According to the FAA, if more than twenty-five percent of students fail the training, it's the program that is at fault and not the pilots. The FAA wanted to decertify the B-737 training program at Alaska Airlines, making it null and void. The FAA was talked out of it, but a number of the pilots had to retake check rides, including myself.

Unlike the C-9, which was a delight to fly, the B-737, nicknamed "The Mudhen," felt unstable. The controls were hydraulically assisted, which made them feel mushy. It was like trying to balance on a soccer ball. The aircraft flew best using the autopilot. The B-737 community loved it. I kept my opinions to myself.

I was flying the line in Southeast Alaska in the B-737. We had four stops a day, and the Mudhen drivers thought they were something special. I didn't tell them that I flew an average of eight legs a day in the C-9. I just agreed with them. Yes, they were very special indeed, but not me, of course. One day, I was flying with a Captain who said, "Oh, you're former military. The problem with military pilots is you can't Ph*&^ing fly and think at the same time." Thank you, Sir. May I have another?

I was landing at Yakutat, Alaska. It was mid-summer. The approach and landing were nothing special. After I landed, we had a long way to go to get to the ramp. About that time, Captain Jammer grabbed the controls and yelled out, "I've got the aircraft." Then, he slammed on the brakes, bringing us to an abrupt stop about a mile and a half from the ramp. He said, "You have to stop this thing. What if there had been ice on the runway?" After all, it was mid-summer, and there was no ice. Then, he had to add a lot a power to get us moving again. The Mudhen drivers prided themselves on going through a set of brakes in two-thirds the time as normal B-737's —*like brakes don't cost anything?*

We continued on. My landing in Seattle went *thump* but not that bad. I had seen a lot worse from the old "experienced" Mudhen drivers. Captain Jammer got on the public address system and said, "At Alaska Airlines, we try to provide our customers with the best air service possible, but that landing didn't come up to our standards and I apologize." What a *prick*! As it turned out, he was a cowboy.

Note: Cowboy pilots don't follow the rules.

In later years, Captain Jammer would get himself into a death stall coming out of Juneau, Alaska. He took off with the head winds right at limits and then made a one-hundred-and-eighty degree turn. The headwinds turned into tailwinds and put the aircraft out of control. After being upside-down, the pilots recovered the aircraft at about two-hundred feet above the ground. Then, without building up enough energy, Captain Jammer climbed back up and stalled it again.

Captain Jammer was given the Airline Pilots Association Safety Award. That day, we just happened to end up at the same restaurant for lunch. I was off probation and could now speak my mind. I went over to him and said, "Congratulations on your safety award. Too bad you almost killed yourself and everybody else to get it." He knew he had screwed up, and he knew he didn't deserve the award. The look on his face was almost worth it. Revenge: a dish best served cold.

Captain Jammer behaved himself for a while. Then, the cowboy came out of him again. He was with a captain who was on his last flight before retirement. He talked the pilot into buzzing Lake Hood in Anchorage after Approach Control had told them not to. Some circuit breakers in the plane were pulled so alarms wouldn't go off. He retired early.

I could go on and on about the B-737/200, but I won't. By that time, Alaska had a brand new aircraft: the B-737/400. I moved from the 200 to the 400 while still on probation. I thought I was rid of Captain Stomper and the cowboys, but management put Stomper in charge of the B-737/400 program.

Actually, my first four years at Alaska weren't that bad, with only a few exceptions. When my training lock had expired, I bid off the B-737 and over to the MD-80.

Note: A training lock is the period of time you are required to fly an aircraft before you can move to another aircraft. In my case, this represented my transition between the B-737 and the MD-80.

The MD-80

The MD-80 was a C-9 on steroids. They both had the same type rating. While flying the C-9 was a forefinger and thumb flying aircraft, the MD-80 needed a full hand, but not both hands like the C-130.

The first day of class, Captain Zip, the MD-80 Equipment Manager, came in to welcome us. Here is what he said, "I want to welcome all of you to my program. I consider you all to be consummate professionals and I am glad to have you here. I have two of the best MD-80 ground school instructors in the entire industry. I'm not saying that just to say it. I say it because it's true. They know how to spoon feed you the information when you need it. The one thing I ask is that you don't try and get ahead of the program. I don't believe in training boards. If you're having problems, we'll get you the additional training. No one needs to know about it but us. I also have some of the best flight instructors in the industry, but if you are having problems with any of them, come to me sooner rather than later. I don't want little problems to turn into big ones. I have an open door policy. Come in, and see me anytime. Are there any questions?"

Notes: "Consummate: Complete in every detail. Perfect. Extremely skilled and accomplished. Of the highest degree."
"Training Boards: A panel that determines if you get fired or not."

I was looking for the hidden camera. Was this a joke? I had been through two training programs already at Alaska and both were unpleasant to say the least. All that time in the Air Force as an instructor and here, on the B-737, I had been surrounded by clowns.

Ground school was as professional as Captain Zip had said, as was the simulator. In the B-737, there was no real training in the simulator. You had seven check rides followed by a final check ride. In the MD-80, there were seven instructional rides, a check ride and instruction if you needed it on the eighth ride. Finally, I had found a home – one where I was welcome and one where I would stay for the remainder of my career at Alaska Airlines.

Captain Cookem was our instructor for practice takeoffs and landings in the airplane. We went to Moses Lake, Washington for the training. There were four of us on board: the instructor, the two students and the training scheduler. I watered Captain Cookem's and the other student's eyes. Captain Cookem said, "You're through. You passed." The other pilot did pretty well. He had been a fighter pilot. He asked me later, "Do you pull past the intended level off and then let the plane settle back into the altitude?" I said, "Yes." He had been trying to force the yoke over and was causing the aircraft to "porpoise" going up and down. Then, Captain Cookem put the training scheduler in the seat and let him fly. With just a few minutes of our training time, the scheduler got the thrill of his lifetime.

There is a requirement to have a minimum of twenty-five hours of IOE (Initial Operating Experience) with an instructor and passengers on board. The successful completion of IOE allows pilots to fly the line without an instructor – standard operating procedures according to the Federal Aviation Rules. I had twenty-six hours and was cleared to fly the line. I knew my stuff!

I had spent my entire time on the B-737 on reserve. There were two types of reserve: "A" – where you had just one hour from the call to be in the seat in the aircraft, and "B" – where you had four hours, but you were on-call most of the month. From hour to hour and day to day, you would never know when you would fly. As soon as I started flying the MD-80, I held a schedule. The difference between the two was like night and day.

Southwest

During my first year at Alaska, I was called by Southwest Airlines for a job interview. It was after my furlough notice and before the furlough – the end of December 1992. At Southwest, I had four one-on-one interviews. Applicants would receive one of three grades from each. The grades were: "Definitely Hire," "Maybe Hire," and "Don't Hire." One "Don't Hire" and you would be out. The longer an applicant stayed, the more the company liked them. I was the last to leave. It was really kind of fun. I had been interviewed before, and I kind of knew what going on.

There was a good cop and a bad cop. The bad cop was the most fun of all. He asked what I had done in the Air Force, and I told him about flying the C-9. I also told him how it was the best job in the Air Force. He said, "Well, I flew an EC-135 out of Tinker AFB, and I think *that* was the best job in Air Force." *Ambush* – all that psychology kicked in. He was trying to get me to argue with him or get mad to see what my reaction would be. I wasn't going to react no matter how bad a cop he was. I looked him straight in the eye and said, "Isn't that cool that we could both come out of the Air Force and think that we had the best jobs?" He then asked me about instructing. I told him how I loved to train new students, right out of pilot training, to hopefully instill in them my philosophy of flying. He asked, "What is your philosophy of flying?" To which I replied, "Do it safe, get it done, and have fun." Then he got all excited and said, "I have to write that down. What were they again?" I told him safety always comes first. He wrote them down and the mood changed completely. He and I were talking and laughing – a good sign. All four of my interviews resulted in a "Definitely Hire," status. Then my packet went to a central hiring board. There was a retired Air Force Colonel on the board. He said, "He retired as a Major. He's an underachiever." He frisbeed my packet into the "Don't Hire" pile.

Mac was very senior and well-thought-of at Southwest. He called me, drunk, and said, "I talked with all four of the interviewers, and they loved you." Mac thought I had been hired. He had actually given a job application to the bad cop when Southwest wasn't handing them out. You had to know someone to get the application. Mac had helped him get *his* job. Still, I didn't get hired.

Mac went to the Chief of Operations and asked him why I wasn't hired. He went in three times. Mac and the Chief of Operations had flown T-37's together at Mather AFB, California. They had a history. Finally, the Chief of Operations said, "I don't have to tell you or anyone else why your buddy didn't get hired." Then he asked, "What's his name?" He looked in the file and had remembered me. He said everyone really loved me then explained to Mac what had happened.

Mac told him I had four years enlisted time in the Marines, but I hadn't put that on my resume. Mac later told me they love former military and military pilots at Southwest Airlines. My time in Vietnam would have been a huge bonus. He asked me why I hadn't put it down, and I told him I didn't think it was relevant. As it was, it worked out for the best in the long run. Things always do for me. It's almost like I have a Guardian Angel.

The fact that I didn't get hired hurt Mac deeply. He used it as an excuse to get drunk. In Sacramento one night, he got busted for a DUI. He told me later that he was concentrating so hard on *not* hitting the median on his left turn that he failed to see the CHP directly in front of him, going in the opposite direction or the red light he drove through. He did, however, see all the bright red and blue lights in his rearview mirror. The CHP read Mac his rights. He said at first the cops were really friendly with him, good cops. All Mac said was, "I want to speak with an attorney, and I want to talk to my union representative." He had to repeat it three times. The cops changed their friendly behavior and got a little mean. After all, he wasn't that drunk. An old friend hooked him up with one of the best criminal defense attorneys in all of Los Angeles. The attorney went into the courtroom and the judge recognized him. He asked, "What are you doing here? This is a simple, one-time DUI charge." Mac got off with two years' probation. If he didn't get into trouble in that time, all record of the DUI would be erased. He also had to go into rehabilitation. The call to the union representative was to admit he had a problem and wanted to go into the HIMS program.

The FAA had set up a program called HIMS (Human Intervention Motivation Study). Prior to the program, if a pilot was diagnosed as an alcoholic, they were permanently grounded for life. The program was to help alcoholics and was later expanded to include drug use. The HIMS program has a ninety-three percent success rate. This, compared to a thirty-three percent success rate of the best civilian programs.

"HIMS is an occupational substance abuse treatment program, specific to treat commercial pilots, that coordinates the identification, treatment, and return to work process for affected aviators. It is an industry-wide effort in which managers, pilots, healthcare professionals, and the FAA work together to preserve careers and enhance air safety." ~ ALPA.

At Alaska Airlines, I worked on the committee for seven years and chaired it for three. Mac was in the program as an offender, and I was helping as a peer counselor. We were not in an adversarial roll.

Mac went into rehabilitation for fifteen months. Normal rehabilitation would take six. When Mac was hired at Southwest, he had signed up for a Loss of Medical insurance coverage and forgotten all about it. When his sick leave and vacation time were used up, he started to get paid his full normal salary through the medical insurance. This, while staying at home and playing with his kids. He was getting even with Southwest for not hiring me.

Flying-the-Line

Captain Cookem was an FAA check designee. He could administer check rides to everyone. As such, he didn't get to fly the line that much. He showed up at the airplane one morning and bumped the captain so he could fly with me. Normally, when *staff pilots* came out to fly the line, they would do so with an experienced or strong co-pilot. Makes sense, if you think about it.

Notes: "Flying the line," means flying a scheduled flight with passengers on board. "Staff Pilots," pilots who spend a lot of time behind a desk.

As we were flying along, Captain Cookem said to me, "I think I was on your new hire interview panel." I said, "Yes, you were." Captain Cookem said, "I think I voted against you." I said, "I think you did too." He then said, "I think I made a mistake." To which I replied, "I think you did too, but thank you."

Later on, in the same flight, we were going into Phoenix, Arizona. It was summer and hot. There were clear skies, but the wind was blowing in all directions. On final approach, we got a tail wind shear alert. Captain Cookem asked, "What do you think?" In training and on the line with a wind shear alert, you are supposed to execute an immediate missed approach. I said, "I'm okay with it as long as we keep the energy up." We had already added our wind correction, which was seventeen knots. We were allowed twenty. I reached up and moved the airspeed indicator up the additional three knots, without being asked. If we were going to play with the rules, I wanted more airspeed. He agreed with my decision, although he was the captain and normally co-pilots don't move anything without the captain's permission. The tail wind shear alert went away. Shortly thereafter we got a headwind shear alert on short final, which is not as critical. We still continued. As we crossed over the runway threshold, we were thirty knots too fast – the winds and all. This was not a problem. He just needed to pull the power off and let the aircraft slow and settle down. Captain Cookem didn't, and we began to float. We would come close to touching down and then the thermals would lift us up again. This was because of all the extra energy. I was giving him airspeed readouts. To back him up, I was telling him how fast we were going. We floated three times and finally touched down with a heavy thump. This was still not a problem. We had just landed very long. All we had to do was slow down and exit at the end of the runway. Captain Cookem deployed the thrust reversers normally. Then, Captain Cookem saw our gate. It was about forty-five degrees to our right. All of a sudden, I felt the brakes coming on full hard. I thought, *oh no*. The antiskid did its thing. We could feel the aircraft. The brakes on the right side deep-cycled on and off. Each time, the right side of the aircraft would sink. I knew what was going on, because I had done it to myself on an occasion or two. So, I knew. Captain Cookem brought the aircraft to an abrupt stop, and we taxied off the runway. I asked him, "Do you want me to see if they have brake fans here?"

Note: Brake fans are used on the ground to blow high speed, high quantity air across the brakes in case of Hot or Overheated brakes.

He said, "I don't think we'll need them." He hadn't been flying the line enough. In the very short time it took to get to the gate, the brakes were already indicating HOT.

Note: The MD-80/C-9's have a brake temperature indicator in the cockpit. Hot breaks were anything over 205 degrees Celsius. Overheated were anything over 315 degrees Celsius.

I told him we already had hot brakes. You're supposed to put the chocks in and release the brakes. We did that, and it helps to cool the brakes. By the time we ran the After-Parking Checklist, the brakes were indicating 330 degrees Celsius and rising. I told him, "I'm running the Overheated-Brakes Checklist." There is a whole list of procedures you have to go through. You have to get people away from the side of the aircraft – the wheels have fuse plugs that are designed to blowout in case of an overheat situation. (The fuse would prevent the tire from exploding, which would be a very bad thing). The last thing on the checklist is to call the fire department. I asked Captain Cookem, "Do you want me to call the fire department now?" He asked, "Do we have to?" My response was, "Yes, Sir. It's on the checklist."

I then called operations and first asked, "Do you have brake fans here?" The answer was, "No." My next question was if they had a Herman Nelson. In Alaska, we used Herman Nelsons as heaters. If the heat wasn't turned on, they acted like a hot brake fan. Operations had no idea what I was talking about. I said, "We have to get some air on the brakes on the right side of the aircraft."

On the ground in hot locations, we would hook up a ground-based air-conditioning tube. It was about two feet in diameter. This was used to help cool the airplane. I told operations to have maintenance put the auxiliary A/C tube on the right brake truck. Operations said, "If we do that, the aircraft will get hot." To which I replied, "That will be the least of our problems." Maintenance did as requested while I saw the brake temperature gauge go off scale high, well past the 500 degree Celsius mark. I had never seen the gauge go that high before.

It helps to understand where the brake temperature sensors are located on the aircraft. They are in a well, deep inside the brakes. Brakes start to heat up from the point where the two parts, the rotor and the stator, come together. As the heat went into where the probes were located, the auxiliary A/C was cooling from behind. The cool air chased the heat away and dissipated it. We never blew the wheel fuses, and after an inspection, we were on our way.

Yes, we bent a few rules, but no one got hurt. Nothing was damaged, and the folks in the back were never the wiser. A lot of things like this happen in aviation. They just do.

I made a lot mistakes in my flying career, but I had a covenant. By the way, that story was never told to anyone until now. I think Captain Cookem will appreciate that.

Jill and Rocky

I was on Facebook one day when I received a message. It sounded like an old friend. At first, I had no idea who she was. She said we had gone to high school together. She did seem to know a lot about me. Finally, I remembered who she was. Her name was Jill, and we had been buddies in high school. The relationship was not romantic, sexual or anything like that. She was just fun, and I enjoyed her company. She remembered me better than I remembered her, but we reconnected.

One day, as she was sitting next to her computer, located aboard a National Oceanic and Atmospheric Administration ship deep in Antarctica, my face showed up on the screen. A female helicopter pilot was looking over her shoulder and said to Jill, "I know him." Jill asked, "Where do you know him from?" The pilot responded, "He was my instructor in C-130's back at Little Rock AFB." Yes, it was Rocky, the first woman C-130 pilot. She said nice words about me. Being an asshole was always an option and never a requirement. The world is a small place – even smaller now with the internet – and the aviation community is smaller still.

There are many sayings in aviation. One is, "Don't piss off your co-pilot. He or she could be your captain at your next airline." Another is, "You're not a real airline pilot until you have been divorced and furloughed at least once in your career." I didn't want to be a "Real Airline Pilot." I just wanted to play like one at work. Aviation can be a turbulent career field.

Alaska Flight 261
January 31, 2000

The Crash Report stated the following:

"An Alaska Airline McDonnell Douglas MD-83 crashed into the Pacific Ocean about 2.7 miles Southwest of Anacapa Island, California after suffering a catastrophic loss of pitch control. The two pilots, three cabin crewmembers, and 83 passengers on board were killed.

The subsequent investigation by the National Transportation Safety Board determined that inadequate maintenance led to excessive wear and eventual failure of a critical flight control system during flight. The probable cause was stated to be 'a loss of airplane pitch control resulting from the in-flight failure of the horizontal stabilizer system jackscrew assembly's acme nut threads. The thread failure was caused by excessive wear resulting from Alaska Airlines' insufficient lubrication of the jackscrew assembly." ~ National Transportation Safety Board

I said in the beginning that some things would have to remain secret. I will only mention a few here. The remainder are too personal and private. A lot of them make me angry – so very angry. Suffice it to say, there was enough blame to go around for all.

As we were landing in Puerto Vallarta (PVR), we heard Alaska Flight 261 on departure talking with Air Traffic Control. Later that night, we heard about the crash. I received a phone call from my friend Mac. I was surprised to hear his voice and said, "Mac it's good to hear your voice." He was on the verge of tears. He said, "Good to hear my voice? It's good to hear yours." Still holding back his tears, he said, "At first they said it was a B-737, and I thought, okay, maybe it's all right. Then they reported that it was an MD-80, and I panicked. I called Bets and asked if you were there and could we talk." She said, "No, he just flew down to PVR. He won't be back until tomorrow." At that point, she hadn't heard about the crash. By then, Mac was scared shitless and near hysteria. He tried once to place an international long distance phone call from Dallas to PVR and got disconnected just before the call reached my room. So, he called again. He said, "I was going to keep on calling all night long, if need be, until I talked with you and knew you were all right." He said, "I know how things change, and they could have been deadheading you home on that airplane." We talked for a long while, but he didn't want to get off the phone. You could hear the love, concern and deep relief in his voice. He said, "I will call Bets to let her know that you are all right." He was still going on and on about how great it was to hear my voice. I got off the phone and broke into uncontrollable tears as I thought to myself, who am I to have a friend so dear? As I write this, I am bought to tears again.

I received a phone call on April 19, 2007. It was from an hysterical women speaking with a deep southern accent. I could barely understand what she was saying. She said, "Todd, Mike's dead. I came home, and he was dead on the bathroom floor. He was all blue." She continued to blabber on in her southern accent. I sat and thought, "Oh my. How am I going to tell this poor woman she has dialed the wrong number?" I didn't know anyone named Mike. As she continued talking, I played back the tape in my head. She had said, "*Todd*." I never called Mac anything other than Mac. I never ever called him Mike. My best friend, my brother of thirty-two years, was gone at age fifty-five. It was the worst phone call I had ever received. I hope and pray to God that I never get another. He died of a massive heart attack. His left pulmonary artery burst. We had different parents, but we were brothers. We shared a brother's love for thirty-two years. I love and miss my friend. I pray to God for his return, but I will see him again sometime in the future. We will fly again together as we did before, high above the clouds. I was fifty-eight at the time, and I have not fully recovered from it yet. My shrink, Doctor Ruby, said, "You have trouble letting go of things." Some things are worth holding on to.

Upgrade to Captain

I was flying with Captain Chris one month, and I was sandbagging. Sandbagging means that I could have and should have upgraded to captain sooner, but I was sitting in the right seat getting my first choice of schedules every month. I would fly to Mexico and other warm places in winter and along the West coast in the summer. I was sandbagging it and loving my life. Captain Chris was also a check airman. During the first flight of the month, he said, "I've seen your seniority. I know what you're doing, and it's time you upgraded to captain. I'm going to make your life a living hell this month and make you want to be a captain." He did, and I did.

Our retirement pay was based on the high five consecutive earning years of the last ten. Captains make more than first officers – about fifty percent more. I had left a great deal of money on the table to be able to have a lifestyle. It was a choice – a tradeoff. I had chosen wisely, Grasshopper, because now I could upgrade and not be on reserve. I knew I wouldn't get the best schedules, but it was what it was.

Note: For someone who had considered having money such a big deal at one time in my life, it was no longer an issue. I had enough.

In 2002, at age fifty-four, I decided I had enough fun in the right seat. I wanted to upgrade to captain. I could have done it four years earlier on the B-737/200 in Anchorage, but I would have been on reserve the entire time. And it was the B-737/200.

The training then was very easy. In fact, I had been there and done that so many times before. I felt as if I had already passed my check ride and was a captain. We were just going through the motions. Don't get me wrong. I took the training seriously and studied very hard, but all the instructors were super. I had flown with almost all of them at one time or another. They knew me and what I could do.

When it came time for my MD-80 "Type-Ride", which if you will remember I already had from my time in the Air Force, who was my check airman? None other than Captain Cookem, and it was under the worst of all conditions. He was *getting* a check ride from the FAA while *giving* me my check ride. Two check airmen in the simulator at the same time with us. One watching the other and both watching me. Both the co-pilot and I passed. There were a couple of debrief items, and the simulator screwed up once. I had to redo one of the maneuvers. They were really emphasizing what they called "Unstable Approaches on Final." The scenario left us high and with little fuel. When we broke out, we saw the runway. I pulled the power back to idle, pushed the yoke forward towards the ground and landed without a problem. However, I had exceeded the maximum allowable number of feet per minute descent on final. So, they had me do it over again and then debriefed me. Captain Cookem told me to never to it again. I said, "Yes Sir." The thing is, I would do it exactly the same way again if I were in a similar situation. It was safe. In fact, I think it was safer than doing a missed approach with little fuel. I would rather violate a rule than run out of fuel. It's called "Captain's Discretion." What that means is, if the captain thinks, in the interest of safety, their actions will or might violate a rule or a regulation, they can do it. Still, if the FAA doesn't agree with the captain's *discretion*, they could be in a lot of trouble.

Boise Check Ride

I was flying one day in Seattle, when a check airman and an instructor pilot jumped on board my aircraft. They relieved my co-pilot. It was going to be a double check ride – again. The instructor was upgrading to check airman. He would be my co-pilot and give me a line check going to and coming back from Boise, Idaho.

Everything that could possibly go wrong, did go wrong. First, the push back crew only had one marshaler. By company regulation, we needed two. I stopped the airplane and asked operations to get us a second marshaler. Next, after we had set everything up on the control panel for takeoff, Seattle tower changed runways. This happened as we were taxiing out. I had to do a one-hundred-eighty degree turn on the ramp and go to the other runway. I almost forgot to change the takeoff runway on the control panel. If I had not changed the panel, all of our commands would have been reversed. I changed the setting on my panel and advised my co-pilot to reset his.

I was warned that on visual approaches going into Boise, we might get a terrain collision avoidance command but not to worry about it. I did get the warning command. I added a lot of power and started to climb. You need to understand that in the simulator or airplane when you get *this* alarm you react accordingly. It's a big deal – a real big deal, because it keeps you from running into mountains. Although they had warned me, it was a conditioned response on my part. I was climbing. The check airman told me to ignore it. We landed in Boise, and they only had one marshaler, just like in Seattle. So, I stopped the aircraft and told operations to get me another marshaler. Then, we taxied in.

On the return trip, we ran into an icing situation when we were descending into Seattle. On the MD-80, because the engines are on the tail, the power has to be pushed up to get the Ice-Warning-Lights to go out. This is always a good practice but even more so with my company on board. With the power up, it's hard to get the airplane to descend. Air traffic control didn't help. ATC had other traffic and had to keep us up high. Now, we were really high. We had an aircraft below us, going to the parallel runway. I could see that airplane on my left side, but the co-pilot could not. He asked nervously, "Where is he?" I responded, "Down there, where I wish we were." I had already slowed. Finally, I received clearance for the approach. I dirtied the airplane up with gear and maximum flaps. The MD-80, unlike the C-9, only has a maximum flap setting of forty degrees, but they have the same limiting airspeed. I got below one-hundred-eighty knots, dumped the nose of my aircraft and down we went. The way I was flying the airplane was not the way we had been taught at Alaska Airlines. It was the way I had learned to fly in C-9's. At that point, both pilots were becoming a little anxious – particularly, the right seater. But, just as I had learned in the C-9 with my two step approach, we were fine. I landed a little long, so I rolled a little further and didn't cook the brakes. On return to our gate, there was still only one marshaler. I repeated the same request for another. That made three times out of four that operations tried to short me on marshalers. We arrived at the gate, and the check airman said, "Great job," as did the brand new check airman. I told the evaluator captain, "I understand," as I rattled off all the things that happened and had gone wrong. I said, "I know who you communicated with on all the other problems, but who did you talk to about the icing problem?" He got a good laugh out of it and said, "It's getting to be harder to fly the line than to do a simulator check." Then he pulled me aside and asked, "Where did you learn to fly the MD-80 that way?" I told him about the C-9. He said, "I flew the B-727 for a long time, and I knew it could do that. But I never knew the MD-80 could and now I do."

A couple of months later, my co-pilot on that flight went to crew scheduling and told them, "I'm going to give Howe a check ride. Give me the easiest turn you can for him. I've seen what he can do." He got on the plane, and we both laughed. He administrated a check ride from Seattle to Sacramento. On the return leg, I offered him the jump seat again. He just smiled and said, "I'll have a seat in the back, thank you." I thought to myself, it's good to have money in the bank.

My Last Flight of Significance

There I was...The last flight I had of any significance was in March of 2008. We were coming into the Seattle area and were above the waters of the Puget Sound. It was a dark, late night, and there was a wind storm with rain. There is a lot of energy when you add rain to the wind. The storm was knocking out transformers all over the Puget Sound Region. Flashes of light were everywhere. It was not at all unlike that night in Vietnam. We were having a time of it. The wind would hold us like it was giving us a hug. Then, it would release us like a spurned lover. We finally aligned ourselves on final. The winds were right-quartering headwinds and direct crosswinds at the maximum allowable limits. We computed our wind correction and added sixteen knots. On final, the gusts were tossing us about. I told the co-pilot to give me all twenty knots, and he did. Because of the turbulence, the auto-throttles turned themselves off. It was actually better, because the auto-throttles were going forward and backward, and it was making it uncomfortable for all on board. I knew I could do a better job controlling the throttles and aircraft myself, but it meant that I would have to work a lot harder. We put in the crab correction at about three-hundred feet above the ground and fought with the winds to keep the nose heading straight down the runway. We touched down on the right main gear and the left followed. It was a nice, soft, smooth touch-down. Adrenalin will do that for you. We taxied in, and I told the passengers in the back, "The easy part is over. Be careful driving home."

There was a B-757 followed by a B-767 on final behind us. They both executed a missed approach and proceeded to their alternates. We were the last airplane to land in Seattle that night. Then Seattle tower closed the airport.

Now for the rest of the story. Boise was our alternate airport. It is only about ninety minutes away from Seattle. I was on a Voluntary Senior Available trip, paying time-and-a-half. We were paid for what we flew but were paid a minimum of five hours a day. If I had gone to Boise and spent the night, I would have made a lot of money. The first officer had a girlfriend who was living in Boise. So, both of us had very little incentive *not* to go to Boise, other than the people in the back who were trying to get to Seattle. Who knows for what reasons? Some, perhaps important others, maybe not. A sick child? Death in the family? Who knows? But there are always reasons why people come out to fly. It was my job to see that the passengers and crew got to their destination safely. I did that job.

Medical Issues

I always had problems with my sinuses – Sinusitis. In 1996, Doctor Mark preformed a bi-lateral mid-section turbinate restructure. He cut the mid-turbinate's in my nose in half. They were supposed to be soft tissue. He said, "They were like cartilage – hard and rigid after repeated infections."

I remember when I woke up from that surgery, a male nurse asked how I felt. My response was, "PAIN." He said, "Oh, I can take care of that." He gave me a shot of something. He returned a little while later and asked me again how I felt. By then, I was forming sentences. My response that time was, "Still pain." Once again, he gave me a shot, and I passed out. That was a painful operation. Doctor Mark had given me a two week prescription for Percocet. I took it for three days. I was supposed to take one every four hours, which worked fine the first day. Then, at three hours and forty-five minutes, the back of my neck would start killing me with pain. I would wait the additional fifteen minutes and take my next pill. The neck and sinus pain would go away. Then, it became three hours and thirty minutes, and then three hours and fifteen. Each time, I waited the full four hours. I stumbled into the bathroom one day and looked at myself in the mirror. I looked and felt like a freaking drug addict. By the way, I don't understand why people would use Percocet or any other drug in this category for recreation. I felt out of control. Pilots like being in control. I also hated that feeling.

I called Doctor Mark's office and told them to get me something else, or I would stop taking anything or use aspirin. There was a very loud, "No" over the phone. They said, "If you stop taking the drug, your blood pressure will raise, and you will start bleeding. If you take aspirin, it will thin your blood, and you'll start bleeding." I said, "You're going to have to do something."

They gave me a prescription for Vicodin. In place of pushing me down like the Percocet, it lifted me into the air. It was a nice, warm feeling, like I was sitting in front of a blazing fire with a glass of fine red wine – snow quietly falling outside, soft music playing in the background, and my arm around my best girlfriend. I didn't get the withdrawal feelings that I had with the Percocet. But Vicodin was too pleasant. I was off the Vicodin in four days, and I missed it. I put the remainder of the bottle in the bottom drawer of the bathroom cabinet for "just in case." I never did do "just in case." I ended up throwing it all away, a month or so later. After all, it was me who had control over my hand and no one else. Don't ever let anyone kid you. It is a choice you make.

In 2000, I had a bi-lateral frontal sinus exploration – the sinuses above the eyes. Exploration means to open. In laymen's terms, it is called a "Roto Rooter." In 2001, Doctor Mark performed a right frontal exploration.

In 2002, I had another sinus infection. I was on my fourth anti-biotic prescription. The infection wasn't going away. Doctor Mark sat me down and said, "Todd, you have a sinus cell inside your right, frontal sinus cavity. The cell also blocks a portion of the normal opening. The sinus cell has a very small opening of its own. The sinus cell continues to get blocked and infected, and then you get sinusitis." I asked, "Can you do another right exploration?" He said, "No. There is already too much scar tissue, and it just won't work." I asked, "Is there anything we can do?" He said, "Todd, the antibiotics aren't working anymore. This is a condition that, before modern antibiotics, you probably would have died before age thirty-five." I asked again, "What can we do?" He said, "Todd, you have a choice. You can either die, go blind or have another surgery." I laughed, thinking it was one of those things doctors might joke about. He wasn't laughing and said, "If the infection goes into the brain, you will die from encephalitis. If the infection goes into the eye socket, you will wake up one morning blind in that eye. Or, you can have a very different type of surgery. It's called Bi-Lateral Frontal Sinus Obliteration." I like choices. So, I opted for what was behind door number three.

I was sitting down while Doctor Mark explained what the surgery would entail. He was going to cut me from ear to ear above the scalp line. Then he was going to peel my face off down to my frontal sinuses. He was going to cut two holes in the frontal sinuses, one on each side. He was then going to scrape away all the mucosal sinus lining, remove the sinus cell, bone, and any remaining infection. Then he was going to harvest fat from my abdomen and stuff it into my frontal sinuses in the holes he had cut. He would then place a couple of titanium plates over the holes. After all this, he would stretch my face back up to the hairline and staple me back together again. WTF! I said, "You have got to be shitting me, right?" He said, "No, I'm not. In addition, you have to go to the Head of the Otolaryngology Department at the University of Washington Medical School for a second opinion." Hmm…This sounded serious.

I had the surgery a few weeks later. I spent two days in the hospital. There was a machine that had a button I could push to get a shot of pain killers. I used it the first night and day. The second night, I stopped pushing the button. The nurse came in the room the following morning and asked if there was problem with the machine. I said, "No." She said, "You haven't used any pain medication since last night at 10 pm." I told her, "It doesn't really hurt that much, and I would rather have the pain than the drugs."

Doctor Mark gave me a prescription for Vicodin. I only used the Vicodin for two days. I really wasn't in that much pain. So, why use the drugs?

Note: Now, in addition to being a Fat-Head, I was also a Hard-Head, because Doctor Mark had to put in the two titanium patches on my forehead. The operation left the top of my skull numb. So, I was also a Numb-Skull. Some of the decisions I had made earlier in life should have confirmed that already.

In 2000, I had severe pain in my lower back. It was so bad, it prevented me from sitting. My tail bone was killing me. I tried a "whoopee cushion." That sort of worked for a while. Then I found a two-inch memory foam pad from Tempurpedic. The doctors found I had Severe Degenerative Disk Disease and Severe Degenerative Arthritis in my spine, lower and upper back. I flew with both for the next eight years with one degree of pain or another.

In the winter of 2006, I started having problems with fatigue. I had difficulty concentrating and was waking up in the middle of the night, choking to death. Over the following year and a half, it only got worse.

The FAA requires that captains get a first class flight physical every six months. The company and our health insurance would not pay for the physicals. The cost was one-hundred seventy-five dollars apiece at the time. I had to pay for it out of pocket. My PCP (Primary Care Physician) and FAA Doctor were one in the same. A lot a pilots use two different doctors in case they had a problem, but if I had a problem serious enough to ground me, I wouldn't want to be flying. I had worked out a deal with the doctor. I was being monitored for high cholesterol. Every six months, I would have to get it checked through blood tests. The company paid for those. I asked and the doctor agreed to take a blood sample and do my first class physical at the same time. She got paid for the blood test, and I got my physicals for free.

She called me in February of 2008 and said, "Todd, I need to see you right away. There is a problem with your blood work. You'll have to come in." I knew I didn't have HIV or any such nonsense, but I had gone to Mexico a lot and thought I might have picked up one of the many alphabet soup types of Hepatitis. I thought it sounded serious, so I went right over. She sat me down and said, "Todd, you have too many red platelets in your blood." I asked, "Isn't that a good thing?" She said, "No, it indicates you might have sleep apnea." "What's that?" I asked. I was serious. I didn't know what it was. Then she explained, "It's when you stop breathing at night." I said, "Oh yeah, I do that." At that point, she was freaking out. She whispered, "Todd, you can't tell me that." I asked, "Why not?" She said, "Because I will have to ground you right now." My mind started racing. Maybe I shouldn't have had her as my PCP. I asked, "Isn't there another test or something?" She was having an ethical dilemma. She said, "There is a sleep study we can do, but I want you to do it immediately." That was in February 2008.

In December 2007, George W. Bush signed into law the Age Sixty-Five Rule. Prior to that time, airline pilots were required by law to retire at age sixty. I wouldn't be sixty until August of 2008. I jumped up and down with joy. I could work for five more years. Then I said to myself, "I don't want to work for five more years. Maybe until age sixty-two or three, in time to see my son get through college, and to be able to collect Social Society." But in February of 2008, that all changed.

The company had two aircraft types on the property, the B-737 and the MD-80. They were going to retire the MD-80 in 2013. Then, it changed to 2011. Around the same timeframe as my sleep apnea diagnosis, the company announced they were going to retire the MD-80 in early August 2008. It was almost on my birthday. I was approaching sixty years of age. I was going to have to go back to school on the B-737 again. It would have been three plus months of stress and a heavy workload. I was tired, hurting, and it was time.

After my meeting with the Flight Surgeon, I went home and calculated how much sick leave and vacation time I had before December 1, 2008. I calculated that I could leave the middle of July and be paid until the first of December.

I received notification on July 14, 2008 that I would start B-737 training on July 28th. I scheduled an appointment for July 24th for a sleep study. That was my interpretation of the Flight Surgeons "Immediately." I completed the test and the result came back: Severe Sleep Apnea. I stopped breathing over four-hundred times per night. No wonder I was tired and had trouble with my concentration.

My FAA doctor called me in on the 25th and grounded me for sleep apnea. She said, "We can put in a request for a special issuance of your Medical Certificate." She also knew about all the problems with my back. I could have gone to her earlier and been grounded for the problems. Six years earlier, she had given me that option. Whenever I thought I could no longer fly safely, she would pull my Medical. A couple of disks in my back no longer had any cartilage. I wasn't ready before, but by then I was. I still loved the flying, but it was just too hard. Part of being a professional pilot is knowing when you should stop flying. I hurt too much, had sleep apnea, and didn't want to go to training again.

I had finally had enough. The doctor was reluctant at first. Then, I told her, "I guess now would be a good time to tell you about my emotional breakdown in 1991 and the resultant severe clinical depression." She knew that I had a Master's Degree in Psychology and that I knew what I was talking about. She added depression to the list of two, and I was grounded for life.

The FAA sent me a short little letter. I still have it here somewhere. It advised me to never enter the cockpit of another aircraft or I would be subject to fine and imprisonment.

The company didn't want to train all the MD-80 captains on the B-737 and then have us leave in two years. So, they offered an early out incentive. Anyone who retired between November 1, 2008 and March 1, 2009 would receive an additional one-hundred-thousand dollar severance bonus. I had heard there might be a bonus. I asked the Lord for one-hundred and fifty thousand dollars. He countered with one-hundred-thousand dollar and I accepted it. I was going to retire on December 1, 2008 anyway.

The company also said anyone taking the bonus would not get flight benefits for life. That was a deal breaker for me. I petitioned the company. I said there were really two groups of pilots in the buyout: those with time to go and those who were eligible for normal retirement. They finally agreed with my position. I received flight benefits for life. That means if there is a seat available on the airplane, I get to fly for free. If there are two seats, my wife gets to come with me or she could fly by herself.

My last flight was a simple turn from Seattle to Spokane and back. I told the first officer on our way over this might be my last flight. It turned out it was. Completely uneventful. That was in July of 2008. My landing in Spokane was a very slight thump.

Until December 1, 2008, I was getting full pay. That stopped on the first, and I started making about a third of what I made before – the same as when I retired from the Air Force. There was less comradery in the airlines than I had encountered in the Air Force flying squadrons, but I did miss the interaction with the crews and passengers. I was one of those captains that would welcome you aboard.

At my retirement party, I said, "I flew for thirty-two years. In that time, no one got hurt, nothing got bent, and I didn't have to call the FAA and explain myself. It has been a good career and now it is a good time to quit. It was not a solo event, and I would like to thank everyone who helped make it happen. Thank You." And that was that, my flying career was over. Others pilots went on for twenty minutes or more.

Note: By the way, in those thirty-two years of flying, I never once needed to use Algebra, but I did need to do simple math in my head all the time.

Time to Unwind

I experienced the same issues as when I retired from the Air Force with one glaring exception: It wasn't as bad as it was in August 1991. At least, not until I found out my son Christopher wanted to become a Marine Corps Officer. On top of everything else, that did me in. Around February of 2009, my former flight surgeon asked, "Do you finally want some help with that depression?" She had suspected my depression the whole time. She thought I might be bi-polar, because when I went to see her, I was always up-beat. That wasn't the issue. I just had some unresolved, unfinished business in life. By then, I was ready for some help and accepted it. She put me on some Wellbutrin. It seemed to work pretty well.

The company had also given us six months of additional medical insurance. On May 1, 2009, it expired, but I still had my military health insurance. I had been receiving mailers from an insurance program through Tricare, my military health care coverage. I talked with Don M., who had already gotten the coverage. He said, "Todd, they treat us like kings. It's the best health insurance coverage I've ever had." *Oh, sure.* So, I went to a presentation and couldn't believe what I was hearing. It sounded almost too good to be true. It turned out that it was *as* good as or *better* than they had advertised. It is an HMO within Tricare. All the horror stories about HMO's were not true. At least, not in our case.

My prescription for Wellbutrin expired, and my new primary care physician would not renew it. She said, "You need to see a psychiatrist for your new prescription."

Doctor Ruby

Doctor Ruby was my psychiatrist. She was in her late twenties or early thirties. She was from Canada, but I think she was from somewhere like India or the Middle East before that. I didn't really care. She was very beautiful, and she was trying to help me – two points in her favor. I liked her already.

My first meeting with her lasted only thirty minutes. I told her what was going on in my life and the real reason for my depression. She diagnosed me on the spot with Major Depression Disorder. How long did she have to go to school to diagnose that one? I could have told her that. She referred me to a psychotherapist.

I saw the therapist five times. I didn't care much for her. She had a plant that was on the window sill. One day, the plant reached over and touched my head. I said, "Yes, little plant. I like you too." The therapist was amazed. She said she had never seen the plant do that before. The plant would either get closer to the patient or try to get away by hugging the window. And *she* was going to help *me*? *Really*? Still, the plant really did reach over and tap me on my head. It was kind of cool, if you think about it.

That therapist left shortly thereafter. Doctor Ruby called me in for a talk. She was very nervous, her legs swaying, and I could tell she had something to tell me. It was something she didn't want to. Her non-verbal communications were always so expressive. Finally, she said, "The therapist is no longer with us, but I have agreed to see some patients until they hire a replacement. Besides, I think you could benefit more from psychoanalysis than psychotherapy."

I started seeing Doctor Ruby once a week for about five months. Then, they hired a replacement therapist. I saw her six times and then stopped going. Doctor Ruby was monitoring my progress, and I received a call to set up an appointment with her. I walked in and sat down. She said, "I noticed you have stopped seeing the new therapist. Is there a reason?" Now, it was me who was nervous. I had something to tell her. One, I didn't want to tell her, and two, I didn't really know how to. Finally, I said, "I don't want to seem like an elitist or a jerk or anything, but (long pause) I think I'm smarter than she is." Doctor Ruby said, "Todd, I think you're smarter than me." I responded, "Well, I don't, and that will make all the difference."

Note: The reason she thought I was smarter than her was because of the short story I had written about Vietnam and read to her. She asked, "Do you know what you did?" I answered, "No." She went on, "You have acted as your own therapist. Even people with PhD's who have been in the psychiatric field for a long time can't do that."

I started seeing Doctor Ruby again, once a week for the next seven months. We made some real progress. She is a beautiful women, inside and out. Her non-verbal communications were not only telling but funny. She could never tell a lie and get away with it. She was my Guardian Angel for a very short while, and I do miss her so. We used to talk and laugh together. So much laughter. I liked making her laugh.

One day, I had another appointment with Doctor Ruby. I walked into her office and asked her how she was. She said, "Okay." I thought, *Uh oh — something is wrong.* I asked her, "Only okay?" She was really nervous this time. Again, I could tell she wanted to tell me something. We had a somewhat normal session. Then, I could see it coming. I said, "I notice your legs are swaying." Her legs stopped immediately. I continued, "The last time you did this is when the therapist left. Since I'm not seeing a therapist anymore, are you leaving me?" She said, "Yes. You really are good at this, aren't you? I told you that you were smarter than me." Not in the least.

She said she was going to Indiana. I asked if there was a young man involved with her decision. Again, her non-verbal communications gave her away. She said, "Yes. How did you know that?" I couldn't fault her for moving for love. She told me when she was leaving and would continue to see me until she left. During her last three weeks, I saw her ten times. I don't think she wanted to leave any more than I wanted her to go.

I took my son with me on my last visit with her and introduced him. She didn't know I was going to bring him. She was quite taken with him. She had written me a beautiful hand written note. That note is below:

11/17/2011

Todd,

It's been a pleasure to work with you.
Your courage to face the truths of yourself and your life has been inspiring... I know this can be one of the most difficult things to do.
To not know what the love and protection of a father feels like and yet become the father that you have.... I have no words.
Thanks for the laughs, remember not to hide behind the smiles too much... 😊
Take Care. R

Charlie and 1/7

A friend on Facebook had joined a group called 2nd Battalion, 5th Marines (2/5). She asked me to join. You may remember Khe Sanh and the other two communications people that were sent there. I thought if there was a 2/5, then there might be a 1/7. I checked online, and, sure enough, there was one. I added my name to the roster.

About a month later, I received an email from someone I thought was trying to sell me life insurance. His name was "Charles C." I looked at the name and almost deleted the email. Then, my mind started doing a memory search. There were no attachments, so I opened it up. Charlie wrote, "Hey, I was stationed with a Todd Howe in Vietnam in 1968 and 1969. Would that be any relationship to you?" Well, I'll be damned. *Memories are like diamonds and rust.*

I replied, "Yeah, Charlie, it's me. How are you and everything?" That was in the summer of 2010. We exchanged numbers and chatted over the phone. He's from Boston and has a heavy accent. He said, "Todd, come on out to Boston. I'll show you around." Alaska Airlines had recently started to fly to Boston. My wife and I had already planned a trip there to experience the fall colors of New England. I told him we were coming. He was excited, and we got together.

The trip was six days for my wife and seven for me. During the first two days, we went to Lexington and Concord. Do it, if you can, before you die. It is a rich part of our history. The next two days were spent with Charlie and his family, and the last two, driving up the coastline of Maine and then inland. We saw New England in full fall colors.

Upon returning to Boston, Charlie said, "I've got a brother-in-law who works for the airlines, and I know how this non-revenue thing works. So, if you get bumped, give me a call." My wife got the last seat on the plane, and I waved goodbye from the window in the terminal. Then, I called Charlie, and he came out to pick me up.

We went down into his basement cave and talked. It was like we were back in Vietnam again, but now our conversation was all about Vietnam and our returns. He was bitter, angry and had PTSD much worse than me. I received thirty percent disability for my PTSD, and he got a hundred percent. He deserves it. Where I had put Vietnam behind me and closed the door, he hadn't and couldn't.

He felt he was on the Marines Corps team, and they had abandoned him. We talked most of the night. Nightmares that haunt him, even when he is still awake. So many of my friends who went to Vietnam came back that way.

My Friend Mac

I could write an entire book about my friendship with "Mac." Who knows? It may be my next book.

We met at Webb AFB, Texas. It was winter of 1974. We had both requested "Hardship – Early assignment to active duty." Our waivers were approved. He and his wife Sue were looking for a place to stay. They found one right across the street from us. We started training in March 1975 and carpooled together for a year. We loved flying, Porsches, music, good times and laughter. At the completion of pilot training, he was assigned a T-37 in California, and I was assigned to C-130's in Alaska. When I couldn't take the black and snow anymore I would travel –space available – on a military plane from Elmendorf AFB, Alaska to Travis AFB, California. Whenever I called Mac and asked if I could come visit, the answer was always the same: "Hell yes! When are you going to be here, and how long are you staying?" I visited him more than a few times in California. He had never planned on making the Air Force a career. To him, it was just a means to an end. I couldn't fault him for that. He hated the Air Force, and when I told him I was staying in, he got pissed at me – but only for a very short while. We talked on the phone a lot. I was assigned to Little Rock AFB, Arkansas in 1981. He was hired by Southwest Airlines in 1982. As soon as he was hired, he invited me to visit him in Dallas, Texas. I did, and he came to Arkansas on occasion. He gave me a lot of "Special Passenger Tickets," on Southwest. He received the tickets from Southwest when passengers would submit nice comments about him. They were all signed by "Herbert 'Herb' David Kelleher, the co-founder, Chairman Emeritus, and former CEO of Southwest Airlines."

Mac was the Captain one night on a flight with Herb and his wife on board. They were going into the Midland Odessa airport. The plane was hit by a "microburst." It turned the aircraft nearly upside down. Mac did all his pilot stuff, saved himself, the passengers, crew and aircraft.

*Note:"A microburst is a downdraft (sinking air) in a thunderstorm that is less than 2.5 miles in scale. Some microbursts can pose a threat to life and property, **but all microbursts pose a significant threat to aviation.**"National Oceanic and Atmospheric Administration.*

When Herb got off the plane, he said to Mac, "That's why I hire pilots and not computer operators." If you have to save someone's life, besides your own, why not make it the CEO?

When Mac got into trouble with his DUI, Herb knew about it and stood with him all the way. Mac continued his drinking. He never flew drunk, he would use alcohol after a flight. A lot of pilots do. He was actually an excellent pilot.

Mac and his wife Sue used to fight a lot. I wouldn't hear from him for a while and then would call and ask, "Are you and Sue fighting again?" He asked, "How did you know that?" I said, "Because I haven't heard from you, and it's been seven years." He said, "What?" I said, "Every time you and Sue fight, you don't call. This happens every seven years." He didn't believe me but went back and checked his records. It *was* every seven years. Each time they fought, they got closer to divorce. The last time, they were separated for about fifteen months. He called me almost daily. I never tired of hearing his voice on the phone. He would always start with "Hey."You cannot believe how much I miss hearing that, "Hey." They finally got back together again. Six months later, he died. Stress will kill you.

My Friend Mac (right) and me
at the Graduation Dinner.

Winter

In Winter, the river flows at its widest and deepest now, But no longer under its own force. It is being pushed along now by the waters behind it. Continuing on its way to an inevitable merger with the sea. On the mountain there is a snowflake ~ frozen.

My Wife

Spring, Summer, Fall and now Winter.

I wrote the book most times in sequence and other times in sections. My wife was the last section I wrote. She told me, "I'm a private person. You can just leave me out if you want." I don't want to.

We met in college on an arranged blind date. She is three years younger than me. Because of my time in the Marines, she was a senior, and I was only a junior. I told her about my life's plan – what I intended to do: Get my degree, go to pilot training, finish a military career, and then fly for an airline. She was impressed. None of the other guys she dated had a clue – much less a plan.

We went everywhere and did everything together. Then, it was coming close to my graduation. She was still hanging around. I think she was looking for a return on her investment. Finally, one day, I told her she was going marry me and be my wife. I didn't ask. Still, she said, "Yes." I didn't expect that. Well…maybe I did.

Throughout my entire childhood, I had grown up with parents who got drunk and fought every night. It was a battle zone. They were mean and vicious to one another. I thought, if this was what married life was like, I was never going to do it. NEVER.

Yet, there I was, preparing to get married. I graduated and was commissioned a 2nd. Lt. in the United States Air Force, in June of 1974. We were married a month later. I started active duty that November. She helped me get through college and pilot training. She would get up on early weeks at 4 am and fix me breakfast – every single day. She was and is a good woman.

We traveled from Oregon to Texas to Alaska to Arkansas to Hawaii and to Illinois. As I was nearing the completion of my Air Force career, we had two small children.

Marriages go through hard times. It was at that time in our marriage that things got very tough. My wife was always my best friend, my lover, my date, my financial partner, someone I could talk to, my everything – always. We would be carrying on a conversation and a child would tug on her pants, and she would walk away mid-sentence. It was like I wasn't even there. I was hurt, angry, and my delicate male ego was bruised. So, I had an affair with my C-9. I fell in love with her, the mission and the people. She was warm, and she was beautiful. After I retired and left the Air Force behind, I had my emotional breakdown. It was at that time that I had thoughts of leaving my wife and children, but I had a very low opinion of men who married, had two children and then would leave when things got a little tough. Besides, I loved my wife and our children.

So, I swallowed my pride and asked myself, "Who needed Betsy more? Me or the children?" The answer was the children, of course. Do children need their father? YES! It doesn't take a village to raise a child. Its takes a mother and a father. I grew up that day.

I was hired by Alaska Airlines in February 1992. We moved to Washington and purchased a home. We raised our children together in our home for the next twenty years. Our house was big and had a huge playroom. Our son coined it, the Share Toy Room. It was where the children would go to share their toys. Because it was so big, all the class parties were held there. It was also the spot for all-nighters. Chris had four very close friends, and they would play video games all night long. Betsy would get up in the morning and feed them all breakfast. She was helping to raise the four boys along with our son. Only one mother ever thanked her. Oh and one father, but then, I said "thanks" a lot.

I was chatting with Betsy one day saying how sad I was that I couldn't have attended more events and games while the children were growing up. She attended many more of those events than I did. She looked at me and said, "You have made it to as many events as most of the other fathers, and would you tell me which event or game there was that you could have attended and did not?" I thought for a moment and then realized that, although I hadn't made it to all of them, I had in fact made it to all I could.

I was with my children just as I wanted. I was allowed to grow up with them. Sometimes, it's takes a wife and mother to snap you out of your cheap shit so you can see the world as it is. Then have the nerve to tell you.

That is my wife. Why she put up with all the bullshit I gave her over the years, I will never know, but she is a good and wonderful person. Better, perhaps, than I deserve but as good as I got. You would like my wife. Everyone does.

My wife Betsy

My Daughter Trisha
Summer, Fall and Winter.

My daughter was born with her eyes wide open in April of 1986, and they have remained that way all of her life. One day, when she was an infant, she was sitting beside a streamer. It was there for my sinuses. She put her hand out into the steam and was scalded. She looked at the steam again and started to put her hand out, but she took it back. It was a lesson learned early. Fool me once but not twice. As she was learning to crawl, she spilled her water bottle onto a ceramic tile floor. She got herself into a lather. I came into the room and looked at her. She was crying, and I said, "I'm not the one that got you into this mess. You did. Would you like me to help you?" She held up both arms as if to say, "Please." She already understood language. At nineteen months, we were at breakfast. The waitress brought her a balloon. Without us saying or doing anything she said, "Thank You." The waitress nearly dropped her jaw off.

She was never a problem when it came to discipline, drugs, or sneaking out. I think I had her pretty much convinced I'd kill her if she did. She was, however, always a challenge. From an early age, she was pretty sure she was the smartest person in the room. More often times than not, she was right.

I think we put her into a preschool too soon. She was always saying. "Wait-a-me." She was a very likeable little girl, and the teacher and other students helped her. The die had been cast.

She was already reading before she was in preschool. Her mother would read to them both nightly. Sometimes, I would too. To see the look in your children's eyes when you read to them is truly priceless. Their little minds wander off to another place. They are imagining. My daughter realized there were things to know in books, and she wanted to know them.

She was ready to go to kindergarten. She read all the requirements and said, "I can do all that," except when it came to tying her own shoes. She didn't know how and was just sure that she wouldn't be allowed to go to school if she couldn't. I got a 2x4 piece of wood. I put a shoe string on it, and she practiced until she got the basic muscle memory down. Then, we put a pair of shoes on her. She failed the first time but got it the second.

I also realized that she was very high strung. In kindergarten, she wanted a part in a play. It was given to another girl, and Trisha went over and bit the girl hard. Trisha bit me once, and I bit her back real hard. Trisha screamed, yelled and cried. Her mother came in, in a fit. I told her what happened. Trisha never bit me or anyone else after that.

I had been hired by Alaska Airlines at this point. We were going to move to Seattle. She would have to start at a new school. The kids who had been there since kindergarten, one half year, never totally accepted her a one of their own. She was an outsider. Wow!

Trisha was in public school until after the fourth grade. In second grade, they did standardized tests, and she was at the top of her class. In fourth grade, she was a little above average – just what the public schools wanted. It was just like in "Harrison Bergeron," by Kurt Vonnegut, a short story about schools and how the perfect student and grade was a C. Beginning in fifth grade, we began to home school both our children. We joined a home schooling co-op. Home schoolers must have their students tested every year. The public schools only do this every two years. She began to flourish again. By seventh grade, we couldn't keep up with her in Math. So we put her in a math club. She excelled again.

When it came time for High School, we had a dilemma. What should we do? We hadn't locked her away like some home school parents do, but it was time for her to broaden her scope. Would we put her in public or private high school? Trisha found (and together we decided on) a private Christian high school. We weren't sure. We had doubts and reservations. During the summer, Trisha had attended a new student orientation and met some kids. On the first day we dropped her off at the school. A group of girls came running over to her, laughing, and squealing like only little girls can, "Trisha you came!" It was a very warm welcome indeed – a good sign, I think. Later that day, we drove past the public high school she would have attended. It was still summer and warm. We had the windows of the car rolled down. We heard the "F" bomb loudly shouted three times. Kids were smoking on campus. Their pants were hanging down to their knees. _Thank you, Lord!_ I think we made the right choice.

She flourished even more in high school. She became a cheerleader her freshman year and then the cheer captain. She was student body Secretary/Treasurer her Junior and Senior years. She put together school programs and events and worked her butt off seeing them through to completion. Proud? Oh, hell yes, I am! She was on the honor roll every term. The high school years passed by quickly – too quickly. She took her SAT exam and scored a 1410. She could go to just about any school she wanted. One night, she showed up at dinner and said she wanted to go to Baylor in Waco, Texas. I had told both our children I would pay for four years of college, tuition, books, room and board. But Baylor was about twice as expensive as the public colleges in Washington State. I said, "You can go to Baylor, if you want, but the extra tuition will be on you. Besides, you want to major in Communications. Washington State University has the second or third, depending on the year, best-rated communication program in the country: the Edward R. Murrow College of Communication." Trisha left the dining room and went downstairs in a bit of a huff. Emerging the next day, she said, "I going to be a Coug." She decided to join the Washington State Cougars in Pullman, Washington. Smart girl.

We decided we would pay our children for grades. I know a lot of parents are against it. They would say, "They should just want to study and get good grades." Well, it doesn't always out work that way. We paid them both in high school and college. They needed money for stuff, and I didn't believe in giving them an allowance without performance. I also told them, "Any scholarship money you get is your money to do with what you will." They would get so much for A's, less for B's, and nothing for C's. If they got a D, I would not pay them anything at all. If they got an F, they would be fined. If they got a 4.0, I would double everything they would have gotten normally. Trisha earned a 4.0 GPA her first semester in college and more after that. As I sat writing the check, she was thinking, *Wow, I'm really hurting Dad now.* That's right, Baby Girl, hurt me. My plan worked as I had planned it would. She received enough scholarship money to pay for one year of college, and it was her money to keep. She earned it.

She attended a short, summertime class in Pullman and came home between summer and winter semesters. She was like a caged Coug. When she returned that fall, she never came home or looked back. Year round, she went to school, and she graduated in three years. She finished with a cumulative 3.85 GPA from the Honors College and was on the Dean's List every semester. Always competing with me. I graduated in three years with a 3.43 GPA and made the Dean's List a few times. Competitive? Hell, yes she is! She competed, and she *won*. Good for you, Girl. "Good-a-you." I always wanted her to win, and she did.

Note: I gave my daughter a new 2007 Toyota Corolla as a graduation present.

After college, she took a job selling software for an accounting business. For the first time in her life, she was failing. All her hard work was not paying off. What a valuable life's lesson to learn and in the right season of her life! Her boyfriend at the time was working for Shea Home Construction, home builders between San Francisco and Sacramento. There was a job opening. It was being a greeter – the first person you meet when you go to look at homes. The job required a lot of school and a practicum test at the end. She scored a ninety-seven. I didn't ask her "Why not a hundred percent." Not that time.

She was hired by Craig over the objection of Jason. Shea at the time had one-hundred-eighty-six full time employees. The market crashed in 2007, and they started laying people off. They got down to a fulltime staff of seventeen. Trisha was one of them. Her boyfriend was not. They broke up, and he moved back home to live with mommy. Craig packed up and moved to Denver. He wanted Trisha to join him again, building and selling homes. Trisha had seen enough cold and snow to last a lifetime. She elected to stay in California.

Jason, by now, realized he made a mistake about Trisha. She had now branched out from just greeting. She was marketing and a jack of all trades. Although it didn't pay well, she wanted to keep her job. She didn't get a raise in over four years. The company couldn't afford it, but she still had a job. Jason came to her and told her he didn't want to see her burn out. She told him that would not happen.

Later, Craig, her old boss, moved back to the Bay Area. He called Trisha and told her he'd like to have lunch with her – his treat. They got together and Craig explained what he wanted. He wanted Trisha to come work for him again, this time in sales. She had already gotten her Realtors License in her spare time but hadn't used it yet. She decided to jump ship and join Craig. When she told Jason, he totally understood and said it was a good move and time, and Craig would take care of her.

She did move, and Craig did take care of her. She started to sell houses. We got a call from her one day, saying, "I sold my first home." Then she sold another and another. She became the top-selling agent in the entire company nation-wide for a while. In fact, she was in competition with a young man who was working for the same company, building houses about three-hundred yards away from where we live. We met and asked the young man if he knew our daughter, Trisha. Yes, he did. She was nominated for two sales awards for all of Northern California: Rookie of the Year and Top Seller. She finished second in both. She also paid sixty percent of her income in combined state and federal income taxes, paid property tax with her rent check, and sales tax. I guess she'd grown tired of busting her ass so others could sit on theirs. She said, one day, "If I can work, they should be able to come over and clean my house." Trisha was begin-ning to burn out. In addition to selling in the East Bay of San Francisco, she was managing the sales staff at a development called "Mountain House." It was too far from the city, with no infrastructure. It wasn't going well.

She is a total Type A personality, going one hundred and ten percent all the time. I like to kid my wife that Trisha's competitive nature takes after her – *Not!* Trisha takes vacations, traveling to Carnival in Rio, and Santiago, Chile. There was an earthquake while she was in Chile. Still, she loved Chile – but Rio, not so much. She has been to Cambodia, Thailand and Bali. They also had an earthquake while she is is Bali. Perhaps it was a trend – the result of all of her energy. She hiked some trails, did some scuba diving, and played with elephants, giving them baths, feeding them and getting kisses. She has been to Peru and hiked the Inca Trail – a four-day trek up to Machu Picchu. The weather was good and she got to see the mountain. Not all are so lucky. She met some people from Australia and spent time with them during her visit there. She did some scuba diving along the Great Barrier Reef. She has been to Morocco, rode a camel, and slept in a tent in the desert. She has now been on all continents of the world with the exception of Antarctica – another place she longs to visit. Though she had a fear of flying (go figure), she purchased some flight time and got her "Dollar Ride" – flew the airplane and got her palms sweaty. That's how she meets all her fears – head-on. She wants all that life has to offer.

My daughter submitted her two weeks' notice at "Richmond America" the latter part of March 2014. They asked her to stay longer, and she finally left at the end of May. At the farewell party, Craig said, "Trisha is not leaving us. She is only taking a leave of absence. When she returns," he pointed to a desk and chair, "she'll be head of the design center." She didn't seem to care too much about that. She was off — on her way to an around-the-world tour. She was gone for six months, finding herself. She is back now and seems more relaxed. She started selling homes again in the Napa region of California

She is on to more challenges and other adventures in her life. She wears me out with her enthusiasm and zest for life, but I wouldn't have her any other way. She is beautiful.

My Daughter Trisha

My Son Christopher

Summer, Fall and now Winter.

My son was born two days after Christmas in the year 1987. When I was growing up, my mother had told me how inconsiderate parents were that would have a child two days before or after Christmas. Thanks again, Mom.

Unlike his sister, he got to start school from kindergarten on. He was doing okay, but he was the kid that never said anything. Since he wasn't a problem, they left him alone. His grades were, for the most part, average or a little above. Christopher is more like his mother — quiet and peaceful. I married his mother. I like him, but I also knew that, left on his own, he wouldn't do as well. I helped teach him to read. I said, "There are only twenty-six letters in the alphabet. Each one has a sound it makes and together they form words." He was stubborn like me. Reading wasn't fun, and he just wasn't going to do it. *Oh, hell yes, he was!*

I told him if he could figure out all the parts of Mario, a video game, then he could learn to read. I put together some flash cards. I would ask Chris, "What is this letter, and what sound does it make?" The first time through, he didn't do very well at all. The second time, he only missed four. The third time, he got all of them correct. He said, "That wasn't that hard. It was kind of fun." More flash cards would come later in life. He was anything but stupid — just a wee bit lazy. He was not unlike his father at that age, but I wasn't going to let that happen.

He went to public school until the end of the second grade. Then, along with his sister, we began home schooling them. I want to say a little about that. We had children because we wanted them. I was just beginning to hold a flying schedule at Alaska, and I was flying every weekend. If my children stayed in public school, I would never see them. They would be in school while I was home and then home on the weekend when I was flying. With home school, they were in the house, and we got to grow up together.

One day, I saw my son standing up and writing at the island in the kitchen. I asked him, "Is that comfortable?" He responded, "Yes." That was the end of the conversation. In public school, they would have forced him to sit down and write. At the beginning of the sixth grade, we put Chris in a private Christian grade school. He was doing very well at the time. But Valley Christian grade school only went through sixth grade. Toward the end of the school year, the school decided to extend to the eighth grade. We gave him a choice for high school. He decided he wanted to go where his sister was. We had gone to a lot of the home games and a few away since Trisha was cheerleading. Chris had been with us. He started school and did very well. He was the student body Vice President his junior and senior year. He lettered in soccer his junior and senior years and in basketball his junior year. In basketball, he didn't think he would get enough play time his senior year. More than likely, his dream of being like Michael Jorden and drafted into the NBA was perhaps out of reach. He was, after all, a white kid, and he couldn't jump. He met an English teacher there who helped mold his life. He had been an English professor at some college and was appalled at the lack of writing skill among college students. He decided to teach at a small Christian high school to make a difference. Both our daughter and son had classes with him. He challenged them in ways they had never been challenged before – not even by me. He demanded excellence and would accept nothing less. My kids would remark about how easy English was in college because of him. In his senior year, instead of playing basketball, Chris tried out for the drama club. He was in two plays. He got the role of antagonist in "The Princess Bride" and the role of a troubled teen in "Marvin's Room."

He decided to join his sister at Washington State University. During his first two years, he majored in partying and was getting straight A's in that subject. In the fall of 2008, he took a Leadership class in Army ROTC. He would later say, "Finally, I found people I could relate to at school." In May 2009, Chris approached me and finally said, "Dad, I want to pursue becoming a Marine Corps Officer." I was already going through some issues with my retirement from flying, and this didn't help. I knew some things had changed in the Corps, but I also knew it was the Corps, where he could get hurt. My Vietnam War issues were still not resolved at that time. He said, "I was afraid to tell you, because I thought you might not approve." Still, his rational was sound. I told him more than a few times when he was growing up that I wouldn't have had any successes in life, had it not been for the Marine Corps. I had told him a lot about the Corps but nothing about Vietnam – only that I had gone. He wanted direction in his life and thought the Marines might help in that. After all, it helped me.

I wrote earlier about my experience with the Marines and OCS. But now, I found out a lot more about the program. The United States Marine Corps Officers Candidate School receives thousands upon thousands of requests each year to enter OCS. The number that apply to go to the school each year far exceeds the available positions. The Marines accept a maximum of 2,400 applicants per year to "interview" for the opportunity to become Marine Corps Officers. Of that number, they only allow a *maximum* of 1,800 to become Marine Officers. Applicants come from the Naval Academy, Naval ROTC, prior enlisted personnel and directly from college. In my son's case, he was coming by way of college. For him, OCS would consist of two six-week courses during the summer between his junior and first senior year. He would have a second senior year because of the partying. The first six weeks is a pass-fail course. The second six weeks is graded, with a minimum requirement of eighty percent to pass. They were graded on Leadership (fifty percent), Academics (twenty-five percent) and Physical Fitness (twenty-five percent). To say the training is intense is an understatement – Twelve-mile humps at 2 am with hundred-pound back packs, Four to five hours of sleep per night, Fifteen challenges per day (though the staff said only ten to twelve could be accomplished).

Prior to my son leaving for OCS, I told him that there was only one thing he could do to disappoint me: Quit. I told him it was fine if he was not selected or if he decided not to join the Corps after completing the training, but if he quit, I told him not to come home. The thing is, I meant it, and he knew it. He wouldn't have quit anyway. During weeks nine through twelve, the staff reduced the number of candidates to ensure the maximum number is not exceeded and to ensure that both the enlisted and officers evaluators wanted the candidate to become officers. My son passed. He was selected to become a USMC Officer. He was not number one, nor was he last in his class. He received no special awards nor recognition, except for a very proud dad. My wife and I went to Washington D.C. on June 28, 2011. We got in very late, drove across the state of Virginia to stay with some friends from the Air Force, C-9's. We arrived at their home at 1:45 am. Good friends who stayed up with the lights on. We spent a couple of days catching up, driving around, having dinners, and looking at horses. We had a great time.

We also got together with a friend who moved out to Virginia about a year before and lived only about fifteen minutes from my Air Force friends. The next night, we drove to Washington D.C. for our son's graduation – the reason for the trip. By the way, our friends from the Air Force and Seattle both drove across the state and shared with us the celebration of graduation. There was also a girl there from his high school who "just happened to be in the Washington D.C. area" during his graduation. It seemed a strange coincidence, if you ask me. I wonder how that happened?

My son graduated from Washington State University in June of 2011. He was commissioned as a 2nd-Lt in the USMC that August. My fall had come to an end. I was honored to administer the oath of office in a church ceremony attended by about fifty people. He then waited for a class date for The Marines Corps' Basic School (TBS). The Basic School is a six-month, academy-like experience. All Marine Officers attend it – a shared experience beyond OCS. It's an excellent concept. He received a notification in the latter part of February for a class starting on March 8, 2012. He needed a car, and so I gave him my 2003 Toyota Highlander with about fifty-eight thousand miles on it. We then set out on a grand, cross-country adventure: Seattle to Quantico, Virginia, in the middle of winter. We studied four different routes and decided on the most northerly. We left Seattle with rain and the windshield wipers going like crazy. Once we crested the Cascade Mountain Range, we turned them off and never used them again on the entire trip. It was clear skies and dry roads all the way – this, while there were tornadoes, thunder snow and blizzard-like conditions just three hundred miles to our south. We stayed in Butte, Montana; Bismarck, North Dakota; Black Falls, Wisconsin; Lima, Ohio and Winchester, Virginia. As we drove along, I reflected on *my* military career – behind me now – and my son's was just beginning. I thought of the friends I had made, the adventures we had shared, and I handed the baton to my son. We stopped and visited with some Alaska Airlines friends in Chicago and spent the night with the same Air

Force friends in Winchester, Virginia. We had allowed eight days for the trip and were arriving in five. The last leg of the trip was to Washington D.C. – the airport for me and the Marines Corps for my son. As we were driving along on that so very short last leg, I said to my son, "I don't know if it matters to you or not, but I consider you to be a fine young man with a great deal of integrity and I think you will make a good Marine Corps Officer." He didn't say anything for the longest time and then, with choked speech, he said, "It does." There was a long pause, and then he said, "Thank you." I said goodbye to my son that day. After that, he wouldn't be coming home again. Give them wings. Teach them to fly, and … *they will fly away.*

Note: I've heard it said, "I wish I was the person my dog thinks I am." I wished I was the person my son thought I was, and then I become that person.

He attended TBS, finished successfully and got his choice of Military Operations Specialty (MOS). He was going to be a Ground Intelligence Officer. His training was at some obscure base close to Virginia Beach. He didn't get his choice of duty stations. Like so many Marines, he wanted to go to Camp Pendleton, California. After the completion of his training, like his father before him, he was assigned to Twenty-nine Palms, California. So, he set out on another cross country trek. I asked him if he wanted me to join him, but he didn't answer yes or no. The same girl that had been at his graduation ceremony for OCS, accompanied him to Twenty-nine Palms.

Chris was assigned to 1st Tanks at Twenty-nine Palms. Tanks are a dying weapon system, and they no longer are deploying them. Chris could have stayed there, safe and secure, until his commitment was up, but he had heard me tell the stories about how I got my C-9 assignment. So, he back-doored an assignment and was assigned to an infantry battalion. He left for the Middle East in September of 2014. When he arrived at his overseas location, he back-doored another assignment to be a Platoon Sniper Team Commander. He returned safely to U.S. soil in April of 2015. He has a strength of character that few possess. He is a gentleman.

My Son Christopher

Reflections

My flying career had its ups and downs, but I have been blessed beyond all measure. I dreamed it, and the dream came true. I have seen and done things few others can boast. I was allowed to fly many different airplanes. Each had its own way. My favorite, of course, was the C-9. I loved it, the mission and the people – more than I should have, perhaps, but not as long or as much as I wanted too.

> *"Flying is like sex - I've never had all I wanted, but occasionally, I've had all I could stand."* ~ *Stephen Coonts.*

Mothers and fathers interact with sons and daughters differently. As we grew up together, at times I liked my son better and at other times my daughter. A natural course of events, I think. If it is true that opposites attract, then I would be more attracted to my son. He is more like his mother, the woman I married so long ago. My daughter, on the other hand, is too much like me. She is going full speed, all the time. She wears me out, but damn, what an amazing person she is!

I *was* harder on my daughter. Why? Because I saw great potential in her. I would not allow her to accept anything less than a hundred percent. It was not because I did not love her. It was because I do. I knew, at some point in time, she would grow her wings and fly away. It can be hard out there. Although it's not right, it is usually more difficult for women than men. She found this out when a window was broken in her car. She called around to get quotes and then her boyfriend did the same. His quotes were eighty percent the cost of her quotes. Not fair? No, not at all. But as I told our children when they were growing up, "The only fair is at the county. It's in the fall, and I'll take you there." I love and respect both of my children but in different ways.

My son is beautiful. We share a very special relationship. He respects me, and I am taken by his natural compassion and caring for others. That must have come from his mother, because I learned it from him. He told me one day, when he was about seven, that he wanted to grow up to be like me. I told him, "When I grow up, I want to be more like you." He gave me a puzzled look. I hope he can now understand what I meant. We grew up together. He has the strangest habit of actually listening to me. Sometimes I was – and still am – amazed by it all. Unlike his sister, he is not a natural A-personality type. But when he wants something, when he dreams it, he can make it come true. Why? Because he works hard for it. Becoming an officer in the Marine Corps is a prime example of that. He will always land on his feet. He is truly an outstanding individual.

Though I was stern with both, I never laid hands on either – unlike my own childhood.

I told my wife, "I wish our children loved me as much as they do you." She said, "I wish they respected me as much as they do you."

"As a rule, man is a fool. When it is hot, he wants it cool. When it is cool, he wants it hot. Always wanting what is not." ~ Anonymous

In this, the winter of my seasons, the pain of not flying diminishes each day. The task of seeing our children grow into the beautiful young people they are is complete. I have fulfilled my commitment and the joy of raising them. I could not be prouder of either.

For a great deal of my life, I always lived looking forward. That changed at the end of my last "Summer of 42" – at age 43, when I entered the Fall of my seasons.

At some point, I looked back upon the path I had traveled and realized there were more bricks behind me now, than in front. I paused, looked and then noticed that all the bricks touched one another. Therefore, as I have touched one, I have, in fact, touched them all. In turn, they have all touched me, and so it is. For those who have touched me so dearly and deeply, I can only say, "Thank you, and I love you!"

Do I have any regrets on the path I have traveled? Of course. Who among us can say we have traveled a perfect path? Only One – and that certainly is not me. People are human, and we make mistakes. I made mistakes – more than a few – some of which I deeply regret. Still, I also made good choices, and I had a Guardian Angel with me always. People helped me along the way, and I thank them for it. Even those who hurt me, helped.

How do I spend my time now? Do I sit on my dead ass in my easy chair, watching some mindless nothing on television? Not hardly! My wife and I travel. One big trip per year. We went to Italy for three weeks in the fall of 2014 to celebrate our fortieth wedding anniversary. Last year, we took a road trip to Southern California. In December 2014, we took another two-week road trip to Las Vegas. I had to see my friend Curt. We used to have coffee together each Saturday morning for about three hours and talk, but he and his wife moved to Las Vegas. We hadn't had coffee for a while, and we needed to talk. You have to work at keeping friendships, and Curt's is worth keeping. We just returned from a seventeen-day road trip to Phoenix for baseball Spring Training. Curt and his wife drove over from Las Vegas, and we got to see for them for three days and two nights. My friend Bill and his wife moved to Spokane and we visit them on occasion. They used to stay with us when they were on this side of the mountain. But since their daughter had a child, they now stay with them. This fall, we are going to the Carolinas. It will be a flying and road trip. We plan to be gone about three weeks. We have already made plans for Spring Training next year.

I work out at the gym three times a week. I get a massage once a week. I am designing and building automobile engines in my shop. I read more than I used to, and of late, I have spent some time writing – not just this book but some short stories. Actually, I prefer the short story *genre* better. One in particular, I wish I could share. It is beautiful – I think the best work I have ever written, but it is too personal and private to share with anyone. I am afraid it could also be hurtful. The Good Wolf wins this battle.

My wife and I are dating again. We are still in love after all these years. I work in the yard, do charity work at the church and spend more time in the Word. I help friends from church repair their cars. My life is and has been full. It is said, the true measure of a successful retirement is to ask yourself daily, "How did I ever find the time to do the things I had to do before?" By that measure, my retirement is successful. At some point, I think I may grow older, but there is plenty of time for that still.

In this, the winter of my life, the Bad Wolf has nearly died from starvation. He has not had a full meal for many years now – only an occasional table scrap which reminds me he is still alive and there. On the other hand, the Good Wolf is fat, sassy, has a full coat of fur, and is beautiful.

I am asked if I miss flying to which I reply, "No. It is not something the FAA will ever allow me to do again. So why miss that which I cannot have?" I wish I could apply that same logic and reason to all things in my life, but I have found I cannot.

Maybe I didn't have the world's greatest childhood, it was also not the worst, but the more bitter the root, the sweeter the fruit. I appreciate my successes, accomplishments and achievements more than most. You play the hand you are dealt, not the one you wished you had. I have found that the would-haves, could-haves and should-haves of life, don't mean Jack Shit. What was, was. What is, is. And what will be, will be. There are at times very little we can do about it.

But other times we can dream, and we can work toward the fulfillment of those dreams. Because, after all, dreams do come true.

...and Here I Am."

Epilogue

"Eventually, all things merge into one, and a river runs through it. The river was cut by the world's great flood and runs over rocks from the basement of time. On some of the rocks are timeless raindrops. Under the rocks are the words, and some of the words are theirs. I am haunted by waters."

~ A River Runs Through It, Norman Maclean.

Todd M. Howe

Some of Todd's Favorite Quotes

"You have to be in a mood, so why not
make it a good one." ~ Todd

"Live life like there's no tomorrow, Love like you've never
been hurt, Work like you don't need the money, Dance like
no one is watching. Life isn't about how to survive through
the storm, it's about learning to dance in the rain!" ~ Unk.

"Life is too short to hang out with people
who piss you off." ~ Todd.

"Pass in peace ... knowing you are loved ...
and will be forever." ~ Todd.

"Never underestimate the damage one individual can do
with the aid of willing accomplices, a compliant press and
an ignorant, uninformed and submissive populace." ~ Todd.

"When you are Right and everyone disagrees with
you, it does not make you Wrong." ~ Todd.

"Lord, please, wrap your loving arms around me, and place
your hands over my mouth." ~ Unk. Could have been me.

"Truth is like the sun. You can shut it out for
a time, but it ain't goin' away." ~ Dez.

"If it looks stupid but it works, it ain't stupid." ~ USMC

"In life, there are no 'do-overs'." ~ Unk.

"Do not make friends with an angry man, or you
will learn his ways. Be at peace with all men, as
far as it is in your ability to do so. For where your
treasure is, so will your heart be also." ~ Unk.

"What sunshine is to flowers, smiles are to humanity. These
are but trifles, to be sure, but scattered along life's pathway,
the good they do is inconceivable." ~ Joseph Addison.

"It is better to die on your feet than to live
on your knees." ~ Emiliano Zapata.

"Dream without fear. Love without limits." ~ Unk.

"Don't be so busy making a living that you
forget to make a life." ~ Unk.

"It ain't over till it's over." ~ Yogi Berra.

"Excellence is the result of caring more than others
think is wise, risking more than others think is safe, dreaming
more than others think is practical and
expecting more than others
think is possible." ~ Anonymous.

"Doing a lot of things is never a good substitute
for doing the right things." ~ Unk.

"When you throw dirt, you lose ground." ~ Unk.

"Why does the caged bird sing? For the same reason I smile.
Because we can and it feels good." ~ Todd

"Never accept 'NO' as an answer, but as a challenge." ~ Todd

"No matter how you feel, always get up. Dress up. Show up. And never give up." ~ Unk

"The question is not whether the glass is half empty or half full. The glass is refillable." ~ Unk

Aviation Quotes of the Month

"Pilots: They are cold and steely-eyed. However, they can also be very charming and personable. The average pilot, despite sometimes having a swaggering exterior, is very much capable of such feelings as love, affection, intimacy and caring. These feelings generally just don't involve anyone else." ~ Anonymous.

"The fable of the happy Pilot: Once upon a time, a pilot asked a beautiful princess, 'Will you marry me'? The princess said, "No"! And the pilot lived happily ever after and flew fighters all over the world and drove hot cars and chased skinny, long-legged, big-breasted flight attendants and hunted and fished and went to topless bars and dated women half his age and drank German beer and Captain Morgan and never heard bitching and never paid child support or alimony and kept his house and guns and ate cold leftovers, potato chips and beans and blew enormous farts and never got cheated on while he was at work and all his friends and family thought he was friggin' cool. And he had tons of money in the bank and left the toilet seat up. The End." ~ Unk.

"The good thing about flying solo is it is never boring." ~ Steve Fossett.

"He who demands everything that his aircraft can give him is a pilot. He who demands one iota more is a fool." ~ Anonymous.

"The flight ain't over till you shut the engines down and walk away. Then you look back, and if she ain't bent and she ain't burnin', your flight is over." ~ A very old and experienced pilot.

"Not all birds can fly. What separates the flyers from the walkers is the ability to take off." ~ Carl Sagan.

"Flying is a hard way to earn an easy living." ~ An Old Pilot's Reflection.

"At the end of our lives, whether they are terribly short or satisfyingly long, the things we will regret are not what we did but what we did not do, because we were afraid to try. For us, the risk that some people may associate with flying historic aircraft at airshows is offset by the satisfaction and quality it brings to our lives." ~ Laird.

"An old pilot is one who can remember when flying was dangerous and sex was safe." ~ Attributed to a former Lima flight leader.

"Were' not happy till you're not happy." ~ Perceived motto of the Federal Aviation Administration (FAA).

"I believe the risks I take are justified by the sheer love of the life I lead." ~ Charles A. Lindbergh.

"It's not you're mistake that matters, but it's how you recover that counts." ~ Bill Cherwin.

"One day, long, long ago, there was this pilot who, surprisingly, was not full of shit, but it was a long time ago, and just for one day." ~ Anonymous.

"The brave may not live forever, but the cautious do not live at all!" ~ Sir Richard Branson

"Beware, dear son of my heart, lest in thy new-found power thou seekest even the gates of Olympus. These wings may bring thy freedom but may also come thy death." ~ Daedalus to Icarus.

"Airplanes don't respond to logbooks, lies or legends, only to good headwork and the control inputs we make." ~ Michael Maya Charles.

"You love a lot of things if you live around them, but there isn't any woman and there isn't any horse, nor any before nor any after, that is as lovely as a great airplane." ~ Ernest Hemingway.

"Death is the handmaiden of the pilot. Sometimes it comes by accident, sometimes by an act of God." ~ A. Scott Crossfield.

"The man who flies an airplane…must believe in the unseen." ~ Richard Bach.

"They cashed in their horses for choppers and went tear assin' around the Nam looking for the shit." ~ Apocalypse Now.

"Nobody who gets too damned relaxed builds up much flying time." ~ Ernest K. Gann.

"What kind of man would live where there is no daring? I don't believe in taking foolish chances, but nothing can be accomplished without taking any chance at all." ~ Charles A. Lindbergh.

"There's a lot of Hollywood bullshit about flying. I mean, look at the movies about test pilots or fighter pilots who face imminent death. The controls are jammed or something really important has fallen off the plane, and these guys are talking like magpies. Their lives are flashing past their eyes, and they're flailing around the cockpit. It just doesn't happen. You don't have time to talk. You're too damn busy trying to get out of the problem you're in to talk or ricochet around the cockpit or think about what happened the night of your senior prom." ~ Brigadier General Robin Olds, USAF.

"And let's get one thing straight. There's a big difference between a pilot and an aviator. One is a technician; the other is an artist in love with flight." ~ E. B. Jeppesen.

"Flexible is much too rigid. In aviation, you have to be fluid." ~ Verne Jobst.

"Without my airplane, I am an ordinary man and a useless one - a trainer without a horse, a sculptor without marble, a priest without a god. Without an airplane, I am a lonely consumer of hamburgers." ~ Richard Bach.

"Never fly in the cockpit with someone braver
than you." ~ Richard Herman Jr.

"An airplane might disappoint any pilot, but it'll
never surprise a good one." ~ Len Morgan.

"You'll be bothered from time to time by storms,
fog, snow. When you are, think of those who went
through it before you, and say to yourself, 'what they
could do, I can do'." ~ Antoine de Saint Exupery. .

"The only time an aircraft has too much fuel on board
is when it is on fire." ~ Sir Charles Kingsford Smith.

"Always keep an 'out' in your hip pocket." ~ Bevo Howard.

"If an airplane is still in one piece, don't cheat on it.
Ride the bastard down." ~ Ernest K, Gann."

"A pilot who says he has never been frightened in an
airplane is, I'm afraid, lying." ~ Louise Thaden.

"I was always afraid of dying. Always. It was my fear
that made me learn everything I could about my
airplane and my emergency equipment, and kept
me flying respectful of my machine and always
alert in the cockpit." ~ General Chuck Yeager.

"'Are you ever afraid when you fly?' That's a good question.
Yeah. I'm always a little afraid when I fly. That's what makes
me so damn good. I've seen pilots who weren't afraid of
anything, who would forget about checking their instruments,
who flew by instinct as though they were immortal. I've

pissed on the graves of those poor bastards too. The pilot who isn't a little bit afraid always screws up, and when you screw up bad in a jet, you get a corporal playing taps at the expense of the government." ~ Lieutenant Colonel Bull Meecham, USMC, in Pat Conroy's book, The Great Santini.

"When once you have tasted flight, you will forever walk the earth with your eyes turned skyward, for there you have been, and there you will always long to return." ~ Leonardo da Vinci.

"Aviation is proof that, given the will, we have the capacity to achieve the impossible." ~ Captain Edward Rickenbacker.

"You haven't seen a tree until you've seen its shadow from the sky." ~ Amelia Earhart.

"There is an art, or rather, a knack to flying. The knack lies in learning how to throw yourself at the ground and miss." ~ Douglas Adams.

"Both optimists and pessimists contribute to our society. The optimist invents the airplane, and the pessimist, the parachute." ~ Gil Stern.

"The desire to fly is an idea handed down to us by our ancestors who, in their grueling travels across trackless lands in prehistoric times, looked enviously on the birds soaring freely through space, above all obstacles, on the infinite highway of the air." ~ Wilber Wright.

"If black boxes survive air crashes, why don't they make the whole plane out of that stuff?" ~ George Carlin.

Glossary of Terms

AFB	Air Force Base
AFROTC	Air Force Reserve Officer Training Corps
ATC	Air Traffic Control
ATC	Air Training Command
AWOL	Absent without leave
Box	Flight Simulator
CCK	Ching Chuan Kang Air Base
CHP	California Highway Patrolman
CINC	Commander in Chief
CO	Commanding Officer
Concertina Wire	Barbed wire obstacle
COPD	Chronic obstructive pulmonary disease
Corps	United States Marine Corps
DG	Distinguished Graduate
FMFPAC	Fleet Marine Force, Pacific
FOD	Foreign Object Damage
G	Gravitational Force
Gomers	Viet Cong
GPA	Grade Point Average
Grunt	Infantry
Guardian Angel	Someone who looks over and protects me
Hatch	Doorway
Herk	C-130 Hercules
Hooch	Living Quarters
IED	Improvised Explosive Device (Booby Trap)
KC-135	An air refueler aircraft
Liberty	Off-Base, free time
Lifer	Someone who can't make it outside the Marine Corps
LZ	Landing Zone
MAC	Military Airlift Command
Mac	My best friend

MOS	Military Occupational Specialty
MP	Military Police
MPC	Military Personnel Center
Muse	Someone who presides over the arts and sciences. Personified as a woman, she is the source of inspiration for a creative artist
NCO	Non-Commissioned Officer
NCOIC	Non-Commissioned Officer in Charge
Notams	A written or oral notification issued to pilots before a flight, advising them of circumstances relating to the state of flying.
OCS	Officer's Candidate School
OIC	Officer in Charge
PAS	Professor of Aerospace Studies
PCC	Portland Community College
PCS	Permanent Change of Station
POG	Personnel Other than Grunt
PT	Physical Training
PTSD	Post-Traumatic Stress Disorder
RPG	Rocker Propelled Grenades
RVN	Republic of Vietnam
SAC	Strategic Air Command
Ship for six	Re-Enlist for Six Years
SIE	Self-Initiated Elimination
SOS	Squadron Officer's School
T-43	Boeing 737
TAC	Tactical Air Command
TB	Tuberculosis
TBS	The Basic School
UO	University of Oregon
UPT	Undergraduate Pilot Training
USMC	United States Marine Corps
VA	Veterans Administration

Todd can be followed on Facebook under the name:
Todd Howe, Seattle Washington
or contacted via Email at:
thereIwasandhereIam@gmail.com

Made in the USA
Middletown, DE
07 January 2022